BRAVE NEW WORLD

Aldous Huxley

D0006053

SPARK PUBLISHING

122 Fifth Avenue
New York, NY 10011
www.sparknotes.com

ISBN 978-1-4114-6945-7

Please submit changes or report errors to www.sparknotes.com/errors.

Printed in Canada

10 9 8 7 6 5 4

CONTENTS

CONTEXT   1

PLOT OVERVIEW   5

CHARACTER LIST   9

ANALYSIS OF MAJOR CHARACTERS   13
    JOHN   13
    BERNARD MARX   14
    HELMHOLTZ WATSON   15
    MUSTAPHA MOND   15

THEMES, MOTIFS & SYMBOLS   17
    THE USE OF TECHNOLOGY TO CONTROL SOCIETY   17
    THE CONSUMER SOCIETY   17
    THE INCOMPATIBILITY OF HAPPINESS AND TRUTH   18
    THE DANGERS OF AN ALL-POWERFUL STATE   19
    PNEUMATIC   19
    FORD, "MY FORD," "YEAR OF OUR FORD," ETC.   19
    ALIENATION   20
    SEX   20
    SHAKESPEARE   20
    SOMA   21

SUMMARY & ANALYSIS   23
    CHAPTER 1   23
    CHAPTER 2   26
    CHAPTER 3   28
    CHAPTERS 4–6   32
    CHAPTERS 7–8   36
    CHAPTERS 9–10   39
    CHAPTERS 11–12   41
    CHAPTERS 13–15   44
    CHAPTER 16   47
    CHAPTERS 17–18   51

IMPORTANT QUOTATIONS EXPLAINED   57

KEY FACTS   61

STUDY QUESTIONS   63

HOW TO WRITE LITERARY ANALYSIS   67
    THE LITERARY ESSAY: A STEP-BY-STEP GUIDE   67
    SUGGESTED ESSAY TOPICS   79
    A+ STUDENT ESSAY   80
    GLOSSARY OF LITERARY TERMS   82
    A NOTE ON PLAGIARISM   84

REVIEW & RESOURCES   85
    QUIZ   85
    SUGGESTIONS FOR FURTHER READING   90

CONTEXT

ALDOUS HUXLEY WAS BORN in Surrey, England, on July 26, 1894, to an illustrious family deeply rooted in England's literary and scientific tradition. Huxley's father, Leonard Huxley, was the son of Thomas Henry Huxley, a well-known biologist who gained the nickname "Darwin's bulldog" for championing Charles Darwin's evolutionary ideas. His mother, Julia Arnold, was related to the important nineteenth-century poet and essayist Matthew Arnold.

Raised in this family of scientists, writers, and teachers (his father was a writer and teacher, and his mother a schoolmistress), Huxley received an excellent education, first at home, then at Eton, providing him with access to numerous fields of knowledge. Huxley was an avid student, and during his lifetime he was renowned as a generalist, an intellectual who had mastered the use of the English language but was also informed about cutting-edge developments in science and other fields. Although much of his scientific understanding was superficial—he was easily convinced of findings that remained somewhat on the fringe of mainstream science—his education at the intersection of science and literature allowed him to integrate current scientific findings into his novels and essays in a way that few other writers of his time were able to do.

Aside from his education, another major influence on Huxley's life and writing was an eye disease contracted in his teenage years that left him almost blind. As a teenager Huxley had dreamed about becoming a doctor, but the degeneration of his eyesight prevented him from pursuing his chosen career. It also severely restricted the activities he could pursue. Because of his near blindness, he depended heavily on his first wife, Maria, to take care of him. Blindness and vision are motifs that permeate much of Huxley's writing.

After graduating from Oxford in 1916, Huxley began to make a name for himself writing satirical pieces about the British upper class. Though these writings were skillful and gained Huxley an audience and literary name, they were generally considered to offer little depth beyond their lightweight criticisms of social manners. Huxley continued to write prolifically, working as an essayist and journalist, and publishing four volumes of poetry before beginning to work on novels. Without giving up his other writing, beginning in 1921, Huxley produced a series of novels at an astonishing rate: *Crome Yellow* was published in 1921, followed by *Antic Hay* in 1923, *Those Barren Leaves* in 1925, and *Point Counter Point* in 1928. During these years, Huxley left his early satires behind and became more interested in writing about subjects with deeper philosophical and ethical significance. Much of his work deals with the conflict between the interests of the individual and society, often focusing on the problem of self-realization within the context of social responsibility. These themes reached their zenith in Huxley's *Brave New World,* published in 1932. His most enduring work imagined a fictional future in which free will and individuality have been sacrificed in deference to complete social stability.

Brave New World marked a step in a new direction for Huxley, combining his skill for satire with his fascination with science to create a dystopian (anti-utopian) world in which a totalitarian government controlled society by the use of science and technology. Through its exploration of the pitfalls of linking science, technology, and politics, and its argument that such a link will likely reduce human individuality, *Brave New World* deals with similar themes as George Orwell's famous novel *1984.* Orwell wrote his novel in 1949, after the dangers of totalitarian governments had been played out to tragic effect in World War II, and during the great struggle of the Cold War and the arms race which so powerfully underlined the role of technology in the modern world. Huxley anticipated all of these developments. Hitler came to power in Germany a year after the publication of *Brave New World.* World War II broke out six years after. The atomic bomb was dropped thirteen years after its publication, initiating the Cold War and what President Eisenhower referred to as a frightening buildup of the "military-industrial complex." Huxley's novel seems, in many ways, to prophesize the major themes and struggles that dominated life and debate in the second half of the twentieth century, and continue to dominate it in the twenty-first.

After publishing *Brave New World,* Huxley continued to live in England, making frequent journeys to Italy. In 1937 Huxley moved to California. An ardent pacifist, he had become alarmed at the growing military buildup in Europe, and determined to remove himself from the possibility of war. Already famous as a writer of novels and essays, he tried to make a living as a screenwriter. He had little success. Huxley never seemed to grasp the requirements of the form, and his erudite literary style did not translate well to the screen.

In the late forties, Huxley started to experiment with hallucino-genic drugs such as LSD and mescaline. He also maintained an interest in occult phenomena, such as hypnotism, séances, and other activities occupying the border between science and mysticism. Huxley's experiments with drugs led him to write several books that had profound influences on the sixties counterculture. The book he wrote about his experiences with mescaline, *The Doors of Perception,* influenced a young man named Jim Morrison and his friends, and they named the band they formed The Doors. (The phrase, "the doors of perception" comes from a William Blake poem called *The Marriage of Heaven and Hell.*) In his last major work, *Island,* published in 1962, Huxley describes a doomed utopia called Pala that serves as a contrast to his earlier vision of dystopia. A central aspect of Pala's ideal culture is the use of a hallucinogenic drug called "moksha," which provides an interesting context in which to view soma, the drug in *Brave New World* that serves as one tool of the totalitarian state. Huxley died on November 22, 1963, in Los Angeles.

UTOPIAS AND DYSTOPIAS

Brave New World belongs to the genre of utopian literature. A utopia is an imaginary society organized to create ideal conditions for human beings, eliminating hatred, pain, neglect, and all of the other evils of the world.

The word *utopia* comes from Sir Thomas More's novel *Utopia* (1516), and it is derived from Greek roots that could be translated to mean either "good place" or "no place." Books that include descriptions of utopian societies were written long before More's novel, however. Plato's *Republic* is a prime example. Sometimes the societies described are meant to represent the perfect society, but sometimes utopias are created to satirize existing societies, or simply to speculate about what life might be like under different conditions. In the 1920s, just before *Brave New World* was written, a number of bitterly satirical novels were written to describe the horrors of a planned or totalitarian society. The societies they describe are called dystopias, places where things are badly awry. Either term, utopia or dystopia, could correctly be used to describe *Brave New World.*

PLOT OVERVIEW

THE NOVEL OPENS in the Central London Hatching and Conditioning Centre, where the Director of the Hatchery and one of his assistants, Henry Foster, are giving a tour to a group of boys. The boys learn about the Bokanovsky and Podsnap Processes that allow the Hatchery to produce thousands of nearly identical human embryos. During the gestation period the embryos travel in bottles along a conveyor belt through a factorylike building, and are conditioned to belong to one of five castes: Alpha, Beta, Gamma, Delta, or Epsilon. The Alpha embryos are destined to become the leaders and thinkers of the World State. Each of the succeeding castes is conditioned to be slightly less physically and intellectually impressive. The Epsilons, stunted and stupefied by oxygen deprivation and chemical treatments, are destined to perform menial labor. Lenina Crowne, an employee at the factory, describes to the boys how she vaccinates embryos destined for tropical climates.

The Director then leads the boys to the Nursery, where they observe a group of Delta infants being reprogrammed to dislike books and flowers. The Director explains that this conditioning helps to make Deltas docile and eager consumers. He then tells the boys about the "hypnopaedic" (sleep-teaching) methods used to teach children the morals of the World State. In a room where older children are napping, a whispering voice is heard repeating a lesson in "Elementary Class Consciousness."

Outside, the Director shows the boys hundreds of naked children engaged in sexual play and games like "Centrifugal Bumble-puppy." Mustapha Mond, one of the ten World Controllers, introduces himself to the boys and begins to explain the history of the World State, focusing on the State's successful efforts to remove strong emotions, desires, and human relationships from society. Meanwhile, inside the Hatchery, Lenina chats in the bathroom with Fanny Crowne about her relationship with Henry Foster. Fanny chides Lenina for going out with Henry almost exclusively for four months, and Lenina admits she is attracted to the strange, somewhat funny-looking Bernard Marx. In another part of the Hatchery, Bernard is enraged when he overhears a conversation between Henry and the Assistant Predestinator about "having" Lenina.

After work, Lenina tells Bernard that she would be happy to accompany him on the trip to the Savage Reservation in New Mexico to which he had invited her. Bernard, overjoyed but embarrassed, flies a helicopter to meet a friend of his, Helmholtz Watson. He and Helmholtz discuss their dissatisfaction with the World State. Bernard is primarily disgruntled because he is too small and weak for his caste; Helmholtz is unhappy because he is too intelligent for his job writing hypnopaedic phrases. In the next few days, Bernard asks his superior, the Director, for permission to visit the Reservation. The Director launches into a story about a visit to the Reservation he had made with a woman twenty years earlier. During a storm, he tells Bernard, the woman was lost and never recovered. Finally, he gives Bernard the permit, and Bernard and Lenina depart for the Reservation, where they get another permit from the Warden. Before heading into the Reservation, Bernard calls Helmholtz and learns that the Director has grown weary of what he sees as Bernard's difficult and unsocial behavior and is planning to exile Bernard to Iceland when he returns. Bernard is angry and distraught, but decides to head into the Reservation anyway.

On the Reservation, Lenina and Bernard are shocked to see its aged and ill residents; no one in the World State has visible signs of aging. They witness a religious ritual in which a young man is whipped, and find it abhorrent. After the ritual they meet John, a fair-skinned young man who is isolated from the rest of the village. John tells Bernard about his childhood as the son of a woman named Linda who was rescued by the villagers some twenty years ago. Bernard realizes that Linda is almost certainly the woman mentioned by the Director. Talking to John, he learns that Linda was ostracized because of her willingness to sleep with all the men in the village, and that as a result John was raised in isolation from the rest of the village. John explains that he learned to read using a book called *The Chemical and Bacteriological Conditioning of the Embryo* and *The Complete Works of Shakespeare,* the latter given to Linda by one of her lovers, Popé. John tells Bernard that he is eager to see the "Other Place"—the "brave new world" that his mother has told him so much about. Bernard invites him to return to the World State with him. John agrees but insists that Linda be allowed to come as well.

While Lenina, disgusted with the Reservation, takes enough soma to knock her out for eighteen hours, Bernard flies to Santa Fe where he calls Mustapha Mond and receives permission to bring John and

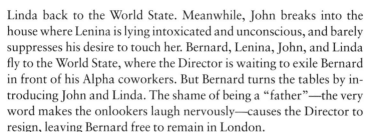

Linda back to the World State. Meanwhile, John breaks into the house where Lenina is lying intoxicated and unconscious, and barely suppresses his desire to touch her. Bernard, Lenina, John, and Linda fly to the World State, where the Director is waiting to exile Bernard in front of his Alpha coworkers. But Bernard turns the tables by introducing John and Linda. The shame of being a "father"—the very word makes the onlookers laugh nervously—causes the Director to resign, leaving Bernard free to remain in London.

John becomes a hit with London society because of his strange life led on the Reservation. But while touring the factories and schools of the World State, John becomes increasingly disturbed by the society that he sees. His sexual attraction to Lenina remains, but he desires more than simple lust, and he finds himself terribly confused. In the process, he also confuses Lenina, who wonders why John does not wish to have sex with her. As the discoverer and guardian of the "Savage," Bernard also becomes popular. He quickly takes advantage of his new status, sleeping with many women and hosting dinner parties with important guests, most of whom dislike Bernard but are willing to placate him if it means they get to meet John. One night John refuses to meet the guests, including the Arch-Community Songster, and Bernard's social standing plummets.

After Bernard introduces them, John and Helmholtz quickly take to each other. John reads Helmholtz parts of *Romeo and Juliet,* but Helmholtz cannot keep himself from laughing at a serious passage about love, marriage, and parents—ideas that are ridiculous, almost scatological in World State culture.

Fueled by his strange behavior, Lenina becomes obsessed with John, refusing Henry's invitation to see a feely. She takes soma and visits John at Bernard's apartment, where she hopes to seduce him. But John responds to her advances with curses, blows, and lines from Shakespeare. She retreats to the bathroom while he fields a phone call in which he learns that Linda, who has been on permanent soma-holiday since her return, is about to die. At the Hospital for the Dying he watches her die while a group of lower-caste boys receiving their "death conditioning" wonder why she is so unattractive. The boys are simply curious, but John becomes enraged. After Linda dies, John meets a group of Delta clones who are receiving their soma ration. He tries to convince them to revolt, throwing the soma out the window, and a riot results. Bernard and Helmholtz, hearing of the riot, rush to the scene and come to John's aid. After the riot is calmed by police with soma vapor, John, Helmholtz, and Bernard are arrested and brought to the office of Mustapha Mond.

John and Mond debate the value of the World State's policies, John arguing that they dehumanize the residents of the World State and Mond arguing that stability and happiness are more important than humanity. Mond explains that social stability has required the sacrifice of art, science, and religion. John protests that, without these things, human life is not worth living. Bernard reacts wildly when Mond says that he and Helmholtz will be exiled to distant islands, and he is carried from the room. Helmholtz accepts the exile readily, thinking it will give him a chance to write, and soon follows Bernard out of the room. John and Mond continue their conversation. They discuss religion and the use of soma to control negative emotions and social harmony.

John bids Helmholtz and Bernard good-bye. Refused the option of following them to the islands by Mond, he retreats to a lighthouse in the countryside where he gardens and attempts to purify himself by self-flagellation. Curious World State citizens soon catch him in the act, and reporters descend on the lighthouse to film news reports and a feely. After the feely, hordes of people descend on the lighthouse and demand that John whip himself. Lenina comes and approaches John with her arms open. John reacts by brandishing his whip and screaming "Kill it! Kill it!" The intensity of the scene causes an orgy in which John takes part. The next morning he wakes up and, overcome with anger and sadness at his submission to World State society, hangs himself.

CHARACTER LIST

John The son of the Director and Linda, John is the only major character to have grown up outside of the World State. The consummate outsider, he has spent his life alienated from his village on the New Mexico Savage Reservation, and he finds himself similarly unable to fit in to World State society. His entire worldview is based on his knowledge of Shakespeare's plays, which he can quote with great facility.

Bernard Marx An Alpha male who fails to fit in because of his inferior physical stature. He holds unorthodox beliefs about sexual relationships, sports, and community events. His insecurity about his size and status makes him discontented with the World State. Bernard's surname recalls Karl Marx, the nineteenth-century German author best known for writing *Capital,* a monumental critique of capitalist society. Unlike his famous namesake, Bernard's discontent stems from his frustrated desire to fit into his own society, rather than from a systematic or philosophical criticism of it. When threatened, Bernard can be petty and cruel.

Helmholtz Watson An Alpha lecturer at the College of Emotional Engineering, Helmholtz is a prime example of his caste, but feels that his work is empty and meaningless and would like to use his writing abilities for something more meaningful. He and Bernard are friends because they find common ground in their discontent with the World State, but Helmholtz's criticisms of the World State are more philosophical and intellectual than Bernard's more petty complaints. As a result, Helmholtz often finds Bernard's boastfulness and cowardice tedious.

Lenina Crowne A vaccination worker at the Central London Hatchery and Conditioning Centre. She is an object of desire for a number of major and minor characters, including Bernard Marx and John. Her behavior is sometimes intriguingly unorthodox, which makes her attractive to the reader. For example, she defies her culture's conventions by dating one man exclusively for several months, she is attracted to Bernard—the misfit—and she develops a violent passion for John the Savage. Ultimately, her values are those of a conventional World State citizen: her primary means of relating to other people is through sex, and she is unable to share Bernard's disaffection or to comprehend John's alternate system of values.

Mustapha Mond   The Resident World Controller of Western Europe, one of only ten World Controllers. He was once an ambitious, young scientist performing illicit research. When his work was discovered, he was given the choice of going into exile or training to become a World Controller. He chose to give up science, and now he censors scientific discoveries and exiles people for unorthodox beliefs. He also keeps a collection of forbidden literature in his safe, including Shakespeare and religious writings. The name Mond means "world," and Mond is indeed the most powerful character in the world of this novel.

Fanny Crowne   Lenina Crowne's friend (they have the same last name because only about ten thousand last names are in use in the World State). Fanny's role is mainly to voice the conventional values of her caste and society. Specifically, she warns Lenina that she should have more men in her life because it looks bad to concentrate on one man for too long.

Henry Foster   One of Lenina's many lovers, he is a perfectly conventional Alpha male, casually discussing Lenina's body with his coworkers. His success with Lenina, and his casual attitude about it, infuriate the jealous Bernard.

Linda   John's mother, and a Beta. While visiting the New
           Mexico Savage Reservation, she became pregnant
           with the Director's son. During a storm, she got lost,
           suffered a head injury and was left behind. A group
           of Indians found her and brought her to their village.
           Linda could not get an abortion on the Reservation,
           and she was too ashamed to return to the World State
           with a baby. Her World State–conditioned promiscuity
           makes her a social outcast. She is desperate to return to
           the World State and to soma.

The Director The Director administrates the Central London
           Hatchery and Conditioning Centre. He is a threatening
           figure, with the power to exile Bernard to Iceland. But
           he is secretly vulnerable because he fathered a child
           (John), a scandalous and obscene act in the World
           State.

The Arch-Community-Songster The Arch-Community-Songster is
           the secular, shallow equivalent of an archbishop in the
           World State society.

Popé   Popé was Linda's lover on the New Mexico Savage
           Reservation. He gave Linda a copy of *The Complete
           Works of Shakespeare*.

The Warden The Warden is the talkative chief administrator for
           the New Mexico Savage Reservation. He is an Alpha.

CHARACTER LIST

ANALYSIS OF MAJOR CHARACTERS

JOHN

Although Bernard Marx is the primary character in *Brave New World* up until his visit with Lenina to the Reservation, after that point he fades into the background and John becomes the central protagonist. John first enters the story as he expresses an interest in participating in the Indian religious ritual from which Bernard and Lenina recoil. John's desire first marks him as an outsider among the Indians, since he is not allowed to participate in their ritual. It also demonstrates the huge cultural divide between him and World State society, since Bernard and Lenina see the tribal ritual as disgusting. John becomes the central character of the novel because, rejected both by the "savage" Indian culture and the "civilized" World State culture, he is the ultimate outsider.

As an outsider, John takes his values from a more than 900-year-old author, William Shakespeare. John's extensive knowledge of Shakespeare's works serves him in several important ways: it enables him to verbalize his own complex emotions and reactions, it provides him with a framework from which to criticize World State values, and it provides him with language that allows him to hold his own against the formidable rhetorical skill of Mustapha Mond during their confrontation. (On the other hand, John's insistence on viewing the world through Shakespearean eyes sometimes blinds him to the reality of other characters, notably Lenina, who, in his mind, is alternately a heroine and a "strumpet," neither of which label is quite appropriate to her.) Shakespeare embodies all of the human and humanitarian values that have been abandoned in the World State. John's rejection of the shallow happiness of the World State, his inability to reconcile his love and lust for Lenina, and even his eventual suicide all reflect themes from Shakespeare. He is himself a Shakespearean character in a world where any poetry that does not sell a product is prohibited.

John's naïve optimism about the World State, expressed in the words from *The Tempest* that constitute the novel's title, is crushed when he comes into direct contact with the State. The phrase "brave new world" takes on an increasingly bitter, ironic, and pessimistic tone as he becomes more knowledgeable about the State. John's participation in the final orgy and his suicide at the end of the novel can be seen as the result of an insanity created by the fundamental conflict between his values and the reality of the world around him.

BERNARD MARX

Up until his visit to the Reservation and the introduction of John, Bernard Marx is the central figure of the novel. Bernard's first appearance in the novel is highly ironic. Just as the Director finishes his explanation of how the World State has successfully eliminated lovesickness, and everything that goes along with frustrated desire, Huxley gives us our first glimpse into a character's private thoughts, and that character is lovesick, jealous, and fiercely angry at his sexual rivals. Thus, while Bernard is not exactly heroic (and he becomes even less so as the novel progresses), he is still interesting to the reader because he is human. He wants things that he can't have.

The major movement in Bernard's character is his rise in popularity after the trip to the Reservation and his discovery of John, followed by his disastrous fall. Before and during his trip to the Reservation, Bernard is lonely, insecure, and isolated. When he returns with John, he uses his newfound popularity to participate in all of the aspects of World State society that he had previously criticized, such as promiscuous sex. This about-face proves Bernard to be a critic whose deepest desire is to become what he criticizes. When John refuses to become a tool in Bernard's attempt to remain popular, Bernard's success collapses instantaneously. By continuing to criticize the World State while reveling in its "pleasant vices," Bernard reveals himself to be a hypocrite. John and Helmholtz are sympathetic to him because they agree that the World State needs criticizing and because they recognize that Bernard is trapped in a body to which his conditioning has not suited him, but they have no respect for him. Lenina's relationship to Bernard is different: she sees him merely as a strange, interesting fellow with whom she can take a break from her relationship with Henry Foster. She is happy to use him for her own social gain, but she doesn't have the emotional investment in him that she does in John.

Helmholtz Watson

Helmholtz Watson is not as fully developed as some of the other characters, acting instead as a foil for Bernard and John. For Bernard, Helmholtz is everything Bernard wishes he could be: strong, intelligent, and attractive. As such a figure of strength, Helmholtz is very comfortable in his caste. Unlike Bernard, he is well liked and respected. Though he and Bernard share a dislike of the World State, Helmholtz condemns it for radically different reasons. Bernard dislikes the State because he is too weak to fit the social position he has been assigned; Helmholtz because he is too strong. Helmholtz can see and feel how the shallow culture in which he lives is stifling him.

Helmholtz is also a foil for John, but in a different way. Helmholtz and John are very similar in spirit; both love poetry, and both are intelligent and critical of the World State. But there is an enormous cultural gap between them. Even when Helmholtz sees the genius in Shakespeare's poetry, he cannot help but laugh at the mention of mothers, fathers, and marriage—concepts that are vulgar and ridiculous in the World State. The conversations between Helmholtz and John illustrate that even the most reflective and intelligent World State member is defined by the culture in which he has been raised.

Mustapha Mond

Mustapha Mond is the most powerful and intelligent proponent of the World State. Early in the novel, it is his voice that explains the history of the World State and the philosophy upon which it is based. Later in the novel it is his debate with John that lays out the fundamental difference in values between World State society and the kind of society represented in Shakespeare's plays.

Mustapha Mond is a paradoxical figure. He reads Shakespeare and the Bible and he used to be an independent-minded scientist, but he also censors new ideas and controls a totalitarian state. For Mond, humankind's ultimate goals are stability and happiness, as opposed to emotions, human relations, and individual expression. By combining a firm commitment to the values of the World State with a nuanced understanding of its history and function, Mustapha Mond presents a formidable opponent for John, Bernard, and Helmholtz.

Themes, Motifs & Symbols

Themes

Themes are the fundamental and often universal ideas explored in a literary work.

The Use of Technology to Control Society

Brave New World warns of the dangers of giving the state control over new and powerful technologies. One illustration of this theme is the rigid control of reproduction through technological and medical intervention, including the surgical removal of ovaries, the Bokanovsky Process, and hypnopaedic conditioning. Another is the creation of complicated entertainment machines that generate both harmless leisure and the high levels of consumption and production that are the basis of the World State's stability. Soma is a third example of the kind of medical, biological, and psychological technologies that *Brave New World* criticizes most sharply.

It is important to recognize the distinction between science and technology. Whereas the State talks about progress and science, what it really means is the bettering of technology, not increased scientific exploration and experimentation. The state uses science as a means to build technology that can create a seamless, happy, superficial world through things such as the "feelies." The state censors and limits science, however, since it sees the fundamental basis behind science, the search for truth, as threatening to the State's control. The State's focus on happiness and stability means that it uses the results of scientific research, inasmuch as they contribute to technologies of control, but does not support science itself.

The Consumer Society

It is important to understand that *Brave New World* is not simply a warning about what *could* happen to society if things go wrong, it is also a satire of the society in which Huxley existed, and which still exists today. While the attitudes and behaviors of World State citizens at first appear bizarre, cruel, or scandalous, many clues point to the conclusion that the World State is simply an extreme—

but logically developed—version of our society's economic values, in which individual happiness is defined as the ability to satisfy needs, and success as a society is equated with economic growth and prosperity.

THE INCOMPATIBILITY OF HAPPINESS AND TRUTH

Brave New World is full of characters who do everything they can to avoid facing the truth about their own situations. The almost universal use of the drug soma is probably the most pervasive example of such willful self-delusion. Soma clouds the realities of the present and replaces them with happy hallucinations, and is thus a tool for promoting social stability. But even Shakespeare can be used to avoid facing the truth, as John demonstrates by his insistence on viewing Lenina through the lens of Shakespeare's world, first as a Juliet and later as an "impudent strumpet." According to Mustapha Mond, the World State prioritizes happiness at the expense of truth by design: he believes that people are better off with happiness than with truth.

What are these two abstract entities that Mond juxtaposes? It seems clear enough from Mond's argument that happiness refers to the immediate gratification of every citizen's desire for food, sex, drugs, nice clothes, and other consumer items. It is less clear what Mond means by truth, or specifically *what* truths he sees the World State society as covering up. From Mond's discussion with John, it is possible to identify two main types of truth that the World State seeks to eliminate. First, as Mond's own past indicates, the World State controls and muffles all efforts by citizens to gain any sort of scientific, or empirical truth. Second, the government attempts to destroy all kinds of "human" truths, such as love, friendship, and personal connection. These two types of truth are quite different from each other: objective truth involves coming to a definitive conclusion of fact, while a "human" truth can only be explored, not defined. Yet both kinds of truth are united in the passion that an individual might feel for them. As a young man, Mustapha Mond became enraptured with the delight of making discoveries, just as John loves the language and intensity of Shakespeare. The search for truth then, also seems to involve a great deal of individual effort, of striving and fighting against odds. The very will to search for truth is an individual desire that the communal society of *Brave New World,* based as it is on anonymity and lack of thought, cannot allow to exist. Truth and individuality thus become entwined in the novel's thematic structure.

THE DANGERS OF AN ALL-POWERFUL STATE

Like George Orwell's *1984,* this novel depicts a dystopia in which an all-powerful state controls the behaviors and actions of its people in order to preserve its own stability and power. But a major difference between the two is that, whereas in *1984* control is maintained by constant government surveillance, secret police, and torture, power in *Brave New World* is maintained through technological interventions that start before birth and last until death, and that actually change what people want. The government of *1984* maintains power through force and intimidation. The government of *Brave New World* retains control by making its citizens so happy and superficially fulfilled that they don't care about their personal freedom. In *Brave New World* the consequences of state control are a loss of dignity, morals, values, and emotions—in short, a loss of humanity.

MOTIFS

Motifs are recurring structures, contrasts, and literary devices that can help to develop and inform the text's major themes.

PNEUMATIC

The word *pneumatic* is used with remarkable frequency to describe two things: Lenina's body and chairs. *Pneumatic* is an adjective that usually means that something has air pockets or works by means of compressed air. In the case of the chairs (in the feely theater and in Mond's office), it probably means that the chairs' cushions are inflated with air. In Lenina's case, the word is used by both Henry Foster and Benito Hoover to describe what she's like to have sex with. She herself remarks that her lovers usually find her "pneumatic," patting her legs as she does so. In reference to Lenina it means well-rounded, balloon-like, or bouncy, in reference to her flesh, and in particular her bosom. Huxley is not the only writer to use the word *pneumatic* in this sense, although it is an unusual usage. The use of this odd word to describe the physical characteristics of both a woman and a piece of furniture underscores the novel's theme that human sexuality has been degraded to the level of a commodity.

FORD, "MY FORD," "YEAR OF OUR FORD," ETC.

Throughout *Brave New World,* the citizens of the World State substitute the name of Henry Ford, the early twentieth-century industrialist and founder of the Ford Motor Company, wherever people in our own world would say Lord" (i.e., Christ). This demonstrates that even at the level of casual conversation and habit, religion has been replaced by reverence for technology—specifically the efficient, mechanized factory production of goods that Henry Ford pioneered.

ALIENATION

The motif of alienation provides a counterpoint to the motif of total conformity that pervades the World State. Bernard Marx, Helmholtz Watson, and John are alienated from the World State, each for his own reasons. Bernard is alienated because he is a misfit, too small and powerless for the position he has been conditioned to enjoy. Helmholtz is alienated for the opposite reason: he is too intelligent even to play the role of an Alpha Plus. John is alienated on multiple levels and at multiple sites: not only does the Indian community reject him, but he is both unwilling and unable to become part of the World State. The motif of alienation is one of the driving forces of the narrative: it provides the main characters with their primary motivations.

SEX

Brave New World abounds with references to sex. At the heart of the World State's control of its population is its rigid control over sexual mores and reproductive rights. Reproductive rights are controlled through an authoritarian system that sterilizes about two-thirds of women, requires the rest to use contraceptives, and surgically removes ovaries when it needs to produce new humans. The act of sex is controlled by a system of social rewards for promiscuity and lack of commitment. John, an outsider, is tortured by his desire for Lenina and her inability to return his love as such. The conflict between John's desire for love and Lenina's desire for sex illustrates the profound difference in values between the World State and the humanity represented by Shakespeare's works.

SHAKESPEARE

Shakespeare provides the language through which John understands the world. Through John's use of Shakespeare, the novel makes contact with the rich themes explored in plays like *The Tempest*. It also creates a stark contrast between the utilitarian simplicity and inane babble of the World State's propaganda and the nuanced, elegant verse of a time "before Ford." Shakespeare's plays provide many examples of precisely the kind of human relations—passionate, intense, and often tragic—that the World State is committed to eliminating.

SYMBOLS

Symbols are objects, characters, figures, and colors used to represent abstract ideas or concepts.

SOMA

The drug soma is a symbol of the use of instant gratification to control the World State's populace. It is also a symbol of the powerful influence of science and technology on society. As a kind of "sacrament," it also represents the use of religion to control society.

Summary & Analysis

Chapter 1

Summary: Chapter 1

The novel opens in the Central London Hatchery and Conditioning Centre. The year is A.F. 632 (632 years "after Ford"). The Director of Hatcheries and Conditioning is giving a group of students a tour of a factory that produces human beings and conditions them for their predestined roles in the World State. He explains to the boys that human beings no longer produce living offspring. Instead, surgically removed ovaries produce ova that are fertilized in artificial receptacles and incubated in specially designed bottles.

The Hatchery destines each fetus for a particular caste in the World State. The five castes are Alpha, Beta, Gamma, Delta, and Epsilon. Gamma, Delta, and Epsilon undergo the Bokanovsky Process, which involves shocking an egg so that it divides to form up to ninety-six identical embryos, which then develop into ninety-six identical human beings. The Alpha and Beta embryos never undergo this dividing process, which can weaken the embryos. The Director explains that the Bokanovsky Process facilitates social stability because the clones it produces are predestined to perform identical tasks at identical machines. The cloning process is one of the tools the World State uses to implement its guiding motto: "Community, Identity, Stability."

The Director goes on to describe Podsnap's Technique, which speeds up the ripening process of eggs within a single ovary. With this method, hundreds of related individuals can be produced from the ova and sperm of the same man and woman within two years. The average production rate using Podsnap's Technique is 11,000 brothers and sisters in 150 batches of identical twins. Called over by the Director, Mr. Henry Foster, an employee at the plant, tells the attentive students that the record for this particular factory is over 16,000 siblings.

The Director and Henry Foster continue to explain the processes of the plant to the boys. After fertilization, the embryos travel on a conveyor belt in their bottles for 267 days, the gestation time period for a human fetus. On the last day, they are "decanted," or born. The entire process is designed to mimic the conditions within a human womb, including shaking every few meters to familiarize the fetuses with movement. Seventy percent of the female fetuses are sterilized; they are known as "freemartins." The fetuses undergo different treatments depending on their castes. Oxygen deprivation and alcohol treatment ensure the lower intelligence and smaller size of members of the three lower castes. Fetuses destined for work in the tropical climate are heat conditioned as embryos; during childhood, they undergo further conditioning to produce adults that are emotionally and physically suited to hot climates. The artificial process, says the Director, aims to make individuals accept and even like "their inescapable social destiny."

The Director and Henry Foster then introduce Lenina Crowne to the students. She explains that her job is to immunize the fetuses destined for the tropics with vaccinations for typhoid and sleeping sickness. In front of the boys, Henry reminds Lenina of their date for that afternoon, which the Director finds "charming." Henry goes on to explain that future rocket-plane engineers are conditioned to live in constant motion, and future chemical workers are conditioned to tolerate toxic chemicals. Henry wants to show the students the conditioning of Alpha Plus Intellectual fetuses, but the Director, looking at his watch, announces that the time is ten to three. He decides there is not enough time to see the Alpha Plus conditioning; he wants to make sure the students get to the Nurseries before the children there have awakened from their naps.

ANALYSIS: CHAPTER 1

Huxley's *Brave New World* can be seen as a critique of the overenthusiastic embrace of new scientific discoveries. The first chapter reads like a list of stunning scientific achievements: human cloning, rapid maturation, and prenatal conditioning. However, the satirical tone of the chapter makes it clear that this technology-based society is not a utopia, but the exact opposite. Like George Orwell's *1984*, *Brave New World* depicts a dystopia: a world of anonymous and dehumanized people dominated by a government made overwhelmingly powerful by the use of technology.

The almost religious regard in which the World State holds technology is apparent from the start. The starting date for the calendar is Henry Ford's introduction of the Model T, an automobile cheaply and efficiently produced by the assembly line system. All dates are preceded by "A.F.," "After Ford," just as today's calendar system begins with the birth of Jesus, A.D. (*Anno Domini,* meaning "in the

year of the lord"). Other satirical hints of a warped religion are
scattered throughout the text. The Predestinators, for example, are
a farcical secular manifestation of the Calvinist religious belief that
God predestines individuals for heaven or hell before birth. The
World State's religious adherence to technology is far from inno-
cent. In fact it becomes one of the pillars of stability for the totalitarian World State. As the Director says, "social stability" is the highest
social goal, and through predestination and rigorous conditioning,
individuals accept their given roles in society without question. The
caste structure is created and maintained using specific tools, and it
is technology that allows the most powerful members of the World
State's ruling Alpha caste to solidify and justify the unequal distribution of power and status.

Conditioning individuals genetically, physically, and psychologi-
cally for their "inescapable social destinies" stabilizes the caste system by creating servants who love and fully accept their servility.
Moreover, conditioning makes them virtually incapable of performing any other function than that to which they are assigned. The
satirical tone of the text makes it clear that, though social stability
may sound like an admirable goal, it can be used for the wrong reasons toward the wrong ends.

One theme emphasized repeatedly in this first chapter is the
similarity between the production of humans in the Hatchery and
the production of consumer goods on an assembly line. Everything
about human reproduction is technologically managed to maximize
efficiency and profit. Following the rule of supply and demand,
the Predestinators project how many members of each caste will
be needed, and the Hatchery produces human beings according to
those figures. One of the keys of mass production is that every part
is identical and interchangeable; a steering wheel from one Model
T fits neatly onto the steering column of any other Ford. Similarly,
in the Hatchery, human beings are standardized by the production
of thousands of brothers and sisters in multiple groups of identical
twins using the Bokanovsky and Podsnap Processes.

The lower castes are more subject to these forces of anonymity
and mechanization. Members of the higher castes are decanted one
by one, without any artificial intervention. Thus the higher castes
retain at least some level of the individuality and creativity that is
denied completely to the lower castes.

CHAPTER 2

SUMMARY: CHAPTER 2

The Director leads the group of students to the Nurseries. Posted on a notice board are the phrases, "Infant Nurseries. Neo-Pavlovian Conditioning Rooms." The students observe a Bokanovsky group of eight-month-old babies wearing the Delta caste's khaki-colored clothes. Some nurses present the babies with books and flowers. As the babies crawl toward the books and the flowers, cooing with pleasure, alarms ring shrilly. Then, the babies suffer a mild electric shock. Afterward, when the nurses offer the flowers and books to the babies, they shrink away and wail with terror.

The Director explains that after 200 repetitions of the same process, the children will have an instinctive hatred of books and flowers. A hatred for books is ingrained in the lower castes to prevent them from wasting the community's time reading books that might "decondition" them. The motivation for instilling a hatred for flowers is more complicated. The Director explains that Gammas, Deltas, and Epsilons were once conditioned to like flowers and nature in general. The idea was to compel them to visit the country often and "consume transport" in the process. But since nature is free, they consumed nothing other than transportation.

In order to increase the consumption of goods, The World State decided to abolish the love of nature while preserving the desire to use transportation. The lower castes are now conditioned to hate the countryside but to love country sports. All country sports in the World State require the use of elaborate apparatus. As a result, the lower castes now pay for both transportation and manufactured goods when they travel to the country for sporting events.

The Director begins to tell a story about a child named Reuben who has Polish-speaking parents. The students blush at the mere mention of the word *parent*. References to sexual reproduction, including words like *mother* and *father*, are now considered pornographic. In the World State, people only use such words in clinical discussions.

The Director continues with his story. One night, Reuben's parents left the radio on while he slept. The child woke up reciting a broadcast of a George Bernard Shaw speech verbatim. The parents did not understand English, so they thought something was wrong. Their doctor understood English and notified the medical press of the event. Reuben's overnight learning led to the discovery of sleep teaching, or hypnopaedia. The Director informs the students that the discovery of hypnopaedia came only twenty-three years after the first Ford Model T was sold. He makes the sign of the T on his stomach (as an observant Catholic might make the sign of the cross) and the students follow suit. He explains that researchers of hypnopaedia soon discovered that it was useless for intellectual training. Reuben could repeat the speech word for word, but had no idea what it meant. The place where hypnopaedia can be used, however, is moral training.

The Director leads the tour to a dormitory where some Beta children are sleeping. The Nurse informs them that the Elementary Sex lesson is over and the Elementary Class Consciousness lesson has just begun. A recorded voice whispers to each sleeping child. It states that Alpha children have to work harder than the other classes and it disparages the lower intelligence and inferiority of the lower castes. The voice teaches pride and happiness in the Beta caste: Betas do not have to work as hard as the cleverer Alphas, it explains, but they are still smarter than the Gammas, Deltas, and Epsilons. The Director explains that the lesson will be repeated one hundred and twenty times, three times a week, for thirty months. Hypnopaedia instills the fine distinctions and prejudices for which electric shocks and alarms are too crude. Hypnopaedia, the Director concludes, is "the greatest moralizing and socializing force of all time."

ANALYSIS: CHAPTER 2
The first half of the students' tour, described in the previous section, illustrates the World State's abuse of biological science in conditioning its citizens. This section focuses on the use of psychological technologies to control the future behavior of World State citizens. Conditioning, combined with prenatal treatment, creates individuals without individuality: each one is programmed to behave exactly like the next. This system allows for social stability, economic productivity within narrow constraints, and a society dominated by unthinking obedience and infantile behavior.

The conditioning technique used to instill a dislike for flowers and books in infants is modeled after the research of Ivan Pavlov, a Russian scientist. Pavlov demonstrated that dogs could be trained to salivate at the ringing of a bell if the sound was consistently visually associated with food. This led to the observation that other kinds of responses could also be conditioned. His work became known to Western science in the decade before *Brave New World* was written.

By applying Pavlovian theory to human infants, the state literally programs human beings to uphold the status quo.

The conditioning also drives the population to support the capitalist economic system. Because the World State wants children to be loyal consumers as adults, the importance of the individual is diminished in order to further the interests of the larger community. Even during their off-work hours, World State citizens serve the interests of production and, therefore, the interests of the whole economy and society, by consuming transportation and expensive sporting equipment. Any opportunity for individual, idiosyncratic behavior that might not feed the economy is eliminated.

CHAPTER 3

Mother, monogamy, romance.

(See QUOTATIONS, p. 57)

SUMMARY: CHAPTER 3

The Director leads the students to the garden, where several hundred naked children are playing. The Director remarks that "in Our Ford's day," games involved no more than a ball or two, a few sticks, and maybe a net. Such simple apparatus did nothing to increase consumption. In the current World State, all games, like "Centrifugal Bumble-puppy," involve complicated machines.

The Director is interrupted by the cries of a little boy sitting in the bushes. It soon becomes clear that the little boy, for some reason, is uncomfortable with the erotic play in which the children are encouraged to participate. After the boy is whisked off to see the psychologist, the Director astounds the students by explaining that sexual play during childhood and adolescence used to be considered abnormal and immoral. When he begins to explain the deleterious effects of sexual repression, a man interrupts him. The Director reverently introduces the man as "his fordship" Mustapha Mond. At the complex, four thousand electric clocks simultaneously strike four, marking the shift change. Henry Foster and Lenina each head up to the changing rooms in preparation for their date. While heading to the rooms, Henry snubs Bernard Marx who is said to have an unsavory reputation.

The narrative suddenly begins to shift back and forth between three different scenes, splicing in Mustapha Mond's speech to the boys with scenes of Henry's conversation in the male changing room and Lenina's conversation in the female training room. This SparkNote will describe Mond's speech first, and then the two changing room conversations.

The students are overwhelmed by meeting Mond, the Resident Controller for Western Europe, and one of only ten World Controllers. Mond quotes Ford, saying, "History is bunk" (an actual quote from the real-life Henry Ford) in order to explain why the students have not learned any of the history that the Director explains to them. The Director glances at him nervously. He has heard rumors that Mond keeps forbidden books, such as Bibles and poetry collections, locked in a safe. Mond, aware of the Director's unease, condescendingly reassures him that he does not plan to corrupt the students.

Mond begins to describe life in the time before the World State began its policy of tight control over reproduction, child-rearing, and social relations. He likens the narrow channeling of emotion and desire to water under pressure in a pipe. One hole produces a strong jet. However, many small holes produce calm streams of water. Strong emotion, inspired by family relationships, sexual repression, and delayed satisfaction of desire, goes directly against stability. Without stability, civilization cannot exist. Before the existence of the World State, the instability caused by strong emotions led to disease, war, and social unrest that resulted in millions of deaths and untold suffering and misery.

Mond describes the initial resistance to the World State's use of hypnopaedia, the caste system, and artificial gestation. But after the Nine Years' War, which involved horrible chemical and biological warfare, an intense propaganda campaign, including the suppression of all books published before A.F. 150, began to weaken the resistance. Religion, Shakespeare, museums, and families all passed into obscurity. The date of the introduction of the Model T was chosen as the start of the new era, and all crosses had their tops cut off to make them into Ts. Six years of pharmaceutical research yielded soma, the perfect drug. The problem of old age was solved, and people could now retain the mental and physical character of youth throughout life. No one was allowed to sit alone and think. No one was allowed "leisure from pleasure."

In the changing room at the end of the workday, Bernard overhears Henry talking with the Assistant Predestinator about Lenina. The Predestinator suggests a "feely" (a movie involving senses of touch and smell) that Henry might want to attend. While discussing Lenina admiringly, Henry tells the Assistant that he should "have her" some time. The conversation disgusts Bernard. The Assistant notices his glum expression and he and Henry decide to bait him. Henry offers Bernard some soma, infuriating him. They laugh as Bernard curses them.

The scene shifts to a public bathroom and showering room, where Lenina is chatting with Fanny Crowne. At age nineteen, Fanny is starting to take a temporary Pregnancy Substitute because she feels "out of sorts." The Pregnancy Substitute mimics the hormonal effects of pregnancy. Fanny expresses surprise that Lenina is still dating Henry exclusively after four months. She advises Lenina to be more promiscuous, as a virtuous member of World State should. Lenina mentions that Bernard Marx, an Alpha Plus hypnopaedia specialist, invited her to the Savage Reservation. Fanny warns that Bernard has a bad reputation for spending time alone and is smaller and less confident than other Alphas. Fanny mentions the rumors that someone might have accidentally injected alcohol into his blood surrogate when he was in the bottle. Lenina decides to accept Bernard's invitation because she thinks Bernard is sweet and wants to see the Reservation. Fanny admires Lenina's Malthusian belt, a contraceptive holder that was a gift from Henry.

ANALYSIS: CHAPTER 3

As the Director and Mustapha Mond explain to the boys how the World State works in an abstract way, the interspliced scenes of Lenina and Bernard show the society in action. The sexual play of the children at recess, the boys' discomfort at the word *mother,* Lenina's relaxed nakedness, and the conversation between Henry and the Predestinator all serve to illustrate how the traditional taboos regarding sexuality have been discarded. Bernard is the sole character to protest—almost silently—the way the system works. His discomfort with the commodification of sex marks him as a misfit. It is worth noting that the novel explicitly establishes that Bernard's dissatisfaction with the State stems from his own isolation within it, introducing Bernard with the words "Those who feel themselves despised do well to look despising." Bernard may be a rebel, but that rebellion does not come from any ideological objection to the World State. It comes from a sense that he might never fully belong to that society. This facet of Bernard's character will be brought into play as the novel progresses.

In addition to prenatal and postnatal conditioning, the World State controls the behavior of its members through the forces of social conformity and social criticism. Lenina's friend Fanny warns her that the Director does not like it when Hatchery workers fail to conform to the expected promiscuity standards. Even as an adult, a World State citizen must fear being seen doing something "shameful" or "abnormal." The adult citizen has no private life. As Lenina notes, the only thing that one does when one is alone in the World State is sleep, and one can't do that forever. In and out of the office, the adult citizen is under surveillance to ensure that his or her body and mind are following the World State's moral value system. Both peers and superiors, like Fanny and the Director, are constantly watching to ensure that each citizen is behaving appropriately.

In his long speech about the history of the World State, Mustapha Mond blames the previously sacred institutions of family, love, motherhood, and marriage for causing social instability in the old society. As Mond explains it, these old institutions shared the work of mediating the conflict between the individual's interests and the interests of society with the State, but the personal institutions and State institutions were themselves out of alignment, creating instability. Individuals cannot always be relied upon to choose the path of most stability since family, love, and marriage produce divided allegiances. Freely acting individuals must constantly weigh the moral value and the moral consequences of their actions. Mond argues that the divided allegiances of individuals produce social instability. For this reason, the World State has eliminated all traces of non-State institutions. The citizen is socialized to only have an allegiance to the State; personal connections of all sorts are discouraged, and even the desire to develop such connections is conditioned away. The constant availability of physical satisfaction evident in the feelies, the abundance of soma, the easy attainment of sex through state sanctioned promiscuity, and the lack of any historical knowledge that might point to an alternate way of life, ensure that the way of life developed and instituted by the World State will not be threatened.

Mustapha Mond and the Director spend a good deal of time discussing the importance of consumption. They are really talking about creating a population that will always want more—a captive market created by conditioning that will want whatever goods the World State produces. This culture of constant consumption allows the government to act as a supplier, propelling the economy and creating a happy community dependent on its supplier. But the economic discussion led by Mond and the Director does not refer only to the economy of money and goods. In *Brave New World*, everything, including sex, operates according to the logic of supply and demand. Citizens are taught to view one another, and themselves, as commodities to be consumed like any other manufactured good. Bernard rebels against this sentiment when he notes that Henry and the Predestinator view Lenina as a "piece of meat"—and that Lenina thinks of herself the same way. Consumption as a way of life is never justified by the World State; it is taken as a way of life.

In Mustapha Mond's discussion of history, *Brave New World* gives some thought to a theme that George Orwell explores in detail in *1984*. Implicit in Mond's statement that "history is bunk" and his discussion of the history of the World State, is the fact that Mond and the other nine World Controllers have a monopoly on historical knowledge. This ensures their positions of power. In *1984*, Orwell describes the mechanisms of this manipulation, as the government of Oceania actively revises history in order to serve its political goals from moment to moment. But in the World State, active revision is unnecessary because the population is conditioned to believe that, as Mond says, "history is bunk." Because they are trained to see history as worthless, they are trapped in the present, unable to imagine alternative ways of life. It is unclear why Mond takes the time to explain the history of the World State to the boys, though it certainly is a convenient way of explaining a possible pathway from the reader's world to that of the World State.

CHAPTERS 4–6

SUMMARY: CHAPTER 4
When Lenina tells Bernard in front of a big group of coworkers that she accepts his invitation to see the Savage Reservation, Bernard reacts with embarrassment. His suggestion that they discuss it privately confuses Lenina. She saunters off to meet Henry. Bernard feels terrible because Lenina behaved like a "healthy and virtuous English girl"— that is, someone unafraid of discussing her sexual life in public. When the genial Benito Hoover strikes up a conversation, Bernard rushes away. Lenina and Henry fly off on their date in Henry's helicopter, and look down upon their world in perfect contentment.

Ordering a pair of Delta-Minus attendants to get his helicopter ready for flight, Bernard betrays his insecurity about his size. The lower castes associate larger size with higher status, so he has trouble getting them to follow his orders. Bernard contemplates his feelings of alienation and becomes irritable. He visits his friend, Helmholtz Watson, a lecturer at the College of Emotional Engineering. Helmholtz is an extremely intelligent, attractive, and properly sized Alpha Plus who works in propaganda. Some of Helmholtz's superiors think he is a little too smart for his own good. The narrator agrees with them, noting that "a mental excess had produced in Helmholtz Watson effects very similar to those which, in Bernard Marx, were the result of a physical defect." The friendship between Bernard and Helmholtz springs from their mutual dissatisfaction with the status quo and their shared inclination to view themselves as individuals. Once together, Bernard boasts that Lenina has accepted his invitation, but Helmholtz shows little interest. Helmholtz is preoccupied with the thought that his writing talent could be better used than simply for writing hypnopaedic phrases. His work leaves him feeling empty and unfulfilled. Bernard becomes nervous, jumping up at one point because he thinks, wrongly, that someone is listening at the door.

SUMMARY: CHAPTER 5

After a game of Obstacle Golf, Henry and Lenina fly in a helicopter over a crematorium where phosphorous is collected from burning bodies for fertilizer. They drink coffee with soma before heading off to the Westminster Abbey Cabaret. They take another soma dose before they return to Henry's apartment. Although the repeated doses of soma have made them almost completely oblivious to the world around them, Lenina remembers to use her contraceptives.

> *Orgy-porgy, Ford and fun,*
> *Kiss the girls and make them One.*
> *Boys at one with girls at peace;*
> *Orgy-porgy gives release.* (*See* QUOTATIONS, *p. 58*)

Every other Thursday, Bernard has to take part in Solidarity Service at the Fordson Community Singery. The participants sit twelve to a table, alternating men and women. While a rousing hymn plays, the participants pass a cup of strawberry ice cream soma and take a soma tablet with it. They work themselves into a frenzy of exultation and the ceremony ends in a sex orgy that leaves Bernard feeling more isolated than ever.

SUMMARY: CHAPTER 6

Lenina convinces Bernard to attend a wrestling match. He behaves gloomily the entire afternoon and, despite Lenina's urging, refuses to take soma. During the return trip, he stops his helicopter and hovers over the Channel. She begs him to take her away from the rushing emptiness of the water after he tells her that the silence makes him feel like an individual. Eventually he takes a large dose of soma, and has sex with her.

The next day, Bernard tells Lenina that he did not really want to have sex with her the first night; he would have preferred to act like an adult instead. Then he goes to get the Director's permission to visit the Reservation. He braces himself for the Director's disapproval of his unusual behavior. When the Director presents the permit, he mentions that he took a trip there with a woman twenty years before. She was lost during a storm and has not been seen since. When Bernard says that he must have suffered a terrible shock, the Director immediately realizes that he has been revealing too much of his personal life. He criticizes Bernard for his antisocial behavior and threatens to exile him to Iceland if his impropriety persists. Bernard leaves the office feeling proud of being considered a rebel.

> *A gramme in time saves nine ... One cubic centimetre cures ten gloomy sentiments ... Everybody's happy nowadays ...*
>
> *(See* QUOTATIONS, *p. 59)*

Lenina and Bernard travel to the Reservation. When they present themselves to the Warden to get his signature on the permit, he launches into a long series of facts about the place. Bernard suddenly remembers that he left the scent tap on at his apartment, an oversight that could end up being extremely expensive. He endures the Warden's seemingly endless speech and then hurries to phone Helmholtz to ask him to turn off the tap for him. Helmholtz has bad news: he tells Bernard that the Director is planning to carry out his threat of exiling him to Iceland. Bernard is no longer proud and rebellious now that the Director's threat has become a reality. Instead, the news crushes and frightens him. Lenina persuades him to take soma.

ANALYSIS: CHAPTERS 4–6

Bernard's role as the protagonist—a role that John will later take over—continues in this section. Increasingly, he appears less like a political rebel and more like a social misfit who believes that changing society is the only way for him to fit in. His conversations with Helmholtz reveal that he is boastful of his liaison with Lenina, afraid of being caught criticizing the World State, and subservient to Helmholtz when it comes to matters of real rebellion. Bernard is a paradoxical character, at one moment lusting after Lenina and at the next hoping that he will have the strength to resist her advances.

Helmholtz, whom we meet for the first time in this section, has the exact opposite of Bernard's problem. Whereas Bernard is too small and strange for his caste, Helmholtz is, if anything, too perfect. His success with women, in his career, and in every other aspect of his life has led him to believe that there must be something more to life than high-tech sports, easy sex, and repetitive slogans. He talks to Bernard because Bernard shares his dislike for the system, but he is aware that Bernard's dislike has a different basis than his own.

The setting of these chapters changes rapidly: from the workplace to Helmholtz's apartment; from Henry's helicopter to Westminster Abbey Cabaret to a crematorium; from Bernard's apartment to the Community Singery; and so on. Some of the scene-shifting is simply used to flesh out a day in the life of a World State member. Lenina and Henry's visit to the Westminster Abbey Cabaret is a blunt joke about the uses to which the World State puts ancient religious sites.

> *Every one works for every one else. We can't do*
> *without any one. Even Epsilons are useful. We couldn't*
> *do without Epsilons.*
>
> *(See* QUOTATIONS, *p. 58)*

As Henry and Lenina contemplate the crematorium, they come close to acknowledging that the caste system may be less than perfect. But then Lenina, troubled and disliking, retreats to one of her stock hypnopaedic phrases, regains her happiness, and the crisis is over. Once again, she is happy to be in her caste and disdainful of those in other castes. This episode, made possible by the setting of a helicopter trip past a crematorium, shows how conditioning can keep the population from questioning the assumptions of the state in which they live. The biggest change in setting is from the World State to the Reservation, though a detailed description of the Reservation is held until the next section.

Although the World State most obviously controls its members by conditioning them and gratifying their desires, there are hints that stability is maintained through methods that are still more sinister. Bernard's sudden fear that someone is listening to his heretical conversation with Helmholtz suggests a totalitarian aspect of the World State. Outside work hours, World State citizens attend strictly regulated, scheduled social activities and never spend any time alone. The lack of time for reflection keeps them occupied and docile. Bernard's fear shows that he is aware of the unwritten but potentially serious consequences of his heretical beliefs.

SUMMARY & ANALYSIS

CHAPTERS 7–8

SUMMARY: CHAPTER 7

At the Reservation, Lenina watches a community celebration. The pounding of the drums reminds her of Solidarity Services and Ford's Day celebrations. The images of an eagle and a man on a cross are raised, and a youth walks into the center of a pile of writhing snakes. A man whips him, drawing blood until the youth collapses. Lenina is horrified.

John, a handsome blond youth in Indian dress, surprises Lenina and Bernard by speaking perfect English. He says that he wanted to be the sacrifice, but the town would not let him. He explains that his mother, Linda, came from the Other Place outside the Reservation. During a visit to the Reservation, she fell and suffered an injury, but was rescued by some Indians who found her and brought her to the village, where she has lived ever since. His father, also from the Other Place, was named Tomakin. Bernard realizes that "Tomakin" is actually Thomas, the Director, but says nothing for the moment.

John introduces Lenina and Bernard to his mother, Linda. Wrinkled, overweight, and missing teeth, she disgusts Lenina. Linda explains that John was born because something went wrong with her contraceptives. She could not get an abortion on the Reservation and felt too ashamed to go back to the World State with a baby. Linda explains that, after starting her new life in the Indian village, she followed all her conditioning and slept with any man she pleased, but some women beat her for taking their men to bed.

SUMMARY: CHAPTER 8

John tells Bernard that he grew up listening to Linda's fabulous stories about the Other Place. But he also felt isolated and rejected, partly because his mother slept with so many men and partly because the people of the village never accepted him. Linda took a lover, Popé, who brought her an alcoholic drink called mescal. She began drinking heavily. Meanwhile, despite being forbidden from taking part in the Indian's rituals, John absorbed the culture around him. Linda taught him to read, at first by drawing on the wall and later using a guide for Beta Embryo-Store Workers that she had happened to bring with her. He asked her questions about the World State, but she could tell him very little about how it worked. One day, Popé brought *The Complete Works of Shakespeare* to Linda's house. John read it avidly until he could quote passages by heart. The plays gave voice to all of his repressed emotions.

Bernard asks John if he would like to go to London with him. He has an ulterior motive that he keeps to himself: he wants to embarrass the Director by exposing him as John's father. John accepts the proposal, but insists that Linda be allowed to go with him. Bernard promises to seek permission to take both of them. John quotes a line from *The Tempest* to express his feelings of joy at finally getting to see the Other World that he had heard about as a child: "O brave new world that has such people in it." Blushing, he asks if Bernard is married to Lenina. Bernard laughs and tells him that he certainly is not. He also cautions John to wait until he sees the World State before he becomes enraptured with it.

ANALYSIS: CHAPTERS 7–8

These chapters contain a crucial plot development: the meeting of Bernard and John. John is an outcast who has always dreamed of living in the World State; Bernard is a World State misfit who is looking for some way to fit in. Their meeting sets in motion a chain of events that produces shattering consequences for both of them.

Huxley uses a literary device called a flashback to bring Bernard, and the reader, up to date on John's background. This device allows Huxley to present a collage of images from John's childhood that would otherwise fit awkwardly into the overall structure of the narrative. If the narrative had been presented in strict chronological order, John and Linda's story would have been told first. Coming in the middle of the novel, it has a greater impact because the reader already knows about the vast differences between World State and Reservation culture. Linda's failure to fit in on the Reservation, and John's confused upbringing, only make sense within the context that has already been provided.

Linda's experiences on the Reservation, as described by herself and by John, demonstrate the extent to which the World State citizens are dependent upon "civilization"—that is, on a life that is completely structured by the state. On the Reservation, she is practically helpless: she does not know how to mend clothing, cook, or clean, and the very idea of taking care of a child horrifies her. She turns to mescal as a poor substitute for soma, which until then had been her only method for dealing with unpleasant situations.

John is a cultural hybrid, absorbing both his mother's culture and that of the Indians on the Reservation. But he is also culturally adrift. The Reservation's community does not accept him, and Linda's Other Place is a distant world he only hears about in stories. So he turns to Shakespeare in his isolation and absorbs a third cultural value system.

Shakespeare's *The Tempest* provides an important parallel to *Brave New World,* and the two texts relate to one another on many levels. In the play, Prospero and his daughter Miranda are exiled to an island because Prospero's brother betrayed him in order to gain political power. The only inhabitant on the Island is a native, Caliban, to whose deceased mother the island had belonged. Prospero usurps control of the island and decides to raise Caliban as a slave because he pities him and intends to civilize him. Shakespeare deftly portrays Caliban as an angry, violent figure, who could easily be interpreted as less than human, ruled by bestial appetites rather than higher instincts. When a ship arrives on the island, two of the stewards introduce Caliban to liquor, and liquor becomes Caliban's "God." Yet Shakespeare also manages to imbue Caliban with all the complexities of the colonized individual. Caliban may be angry and violent, but he has been oppressed by Prospero. Caliban becomes enthralled by liquor and sees it as a god, but he has never seen alcohol before, and the effects of becoming drunk must be staggering to him. Prospero purports to help Caliban by "civilizing" him, but Caliban resents Prospero for the theft of his home. Prospero views Caliban's resentment as unfounded and as evidence of his bestial nature, and this prompts him to treat Caliban even more harshly. Caliban responds with violent action that only increases Prospero's belief that Caliban is an animal. In *The Tempest,* Caliban is both "savage" and a "Noble Savage," he is utterly displaced in every community, just as John is on the Reservation, and will come to be in the World State.

Both *The Tempest* and *Brave New World* can be interpreted as allegories of colonization. Prospero decides to raise Caliban and "civilize" him in the same way that European colonials attempted to "civilize" the African, Asian, and Native American cultures with which they came into contact. For British and other European colonizers, civilizing the savages was a process of replacing native cultures and languages with the culture and language of the colonizer. The colonizers effectively separated colonized peoples from their own history and culture, making it more difficult for the latter to rebel against the new implanted culture that had become their own. The entire World State is built on just such a premise, effacing the past and all its cultural legacies. The World State, in a sense, has colonized everyone.

CHAPTERS 9–10

SUMMARY: CHAPTER 9

Lenina, disgusted by the Reservation, takes enough soma to incapacitate herself for eighteen hours. Bernard flies to Santa Fé to call Mustapha Mond. He repeats his story to a succession of secretaries before finally reaching the World Controller. Mond agrees that John and Linda are a matter of scientific interest to the World State. He instructs Bernard to visit the Warden of the Reservation to pick up the orders that will release John and Linda into his care. Meanwhile, fearful that Bernard and Lenina have left without him, John breaks into the cabin where Lenina is still on soma-holiday. He rifles through her things before he finds her passed out on the bed. He gazes at her, quietly quoting passages from *Romeo and Juliet*. He wants to touch her but fears that it would defile her. As he gazes at her, Bernard's helicopter approaches, and John is able to run from the house and hide his trespass.

SUMMARY: CHAPTER 10

Back at the Hatchery, the Director tells Henry that he plans to dismiss Bernard in front of dozens of high-caste workers as a public example. He explains that Bernard's unorthodox behavior threatens stability. Sacrificing one individual for the greater good of the society is no great loss since the Hatchery can churn out dozens of new babies.

When Bernard arrives, the Director declares Bernard "heretical" because he refuses to behave like an infant and does not immediately seek to gratify his own desires. He tells Bernard that he is being transferred to Iceland. But then Bernard presents Linda and John. Linda accuses the Director of making her have a baby and the room suddenly falls silent. John falls at the Director's feet and cries, "My father!" The workers break out into peals of hysterical laughter as the Director rushes from the room.

ANALYSIS: CHAPTERS 9–10

In these chapters the interlude at the Reservation ends and John's life in the World State begins. The conflict between John's values and the social mores of the World State starts to become obvious. The shift of setting, from the Reservation in New Mexico to the World State in England, foreshadows the shift that is about to take place in the lives of both John and Bernard.

John's character is revealed more fully in his confrontations with World State culture. His struggle to suppress his desire to touch Lenina demonstrates the moral code that he has internalized from Shakespeare and from the "savages" on the Reservation. A World State resident would have gone for instant gratification. John finds himself in the unenviable position of living in the World State without World State conditioning. He is attracted to Lenina, but his views on sex are so radically different from hers that conflict is inevitable. The struggle between John's intense desires and his equally intense self-control is a major facet of his character.

John's habit of quoting lines from Shakespeare's plays not only highlights his distance from World State society, it also serves as a reminder of the distance between our society, in which Shakespeare is revered as a writer with deep insight into human nature, and World State society, in which Shakespeare is unknown and even incomprehensible.

Stylistically, John's Shakespearean quotations contrast vividly with the utterances of the World State citizens. But there is one notable similarity between them. Both the World State citizens *and* John habitually speak in quotes and soundbites. Hypnopaedic messages like "A gramme in time saves nine," are on everybody's lips in the World State. At times the conversations between John and Lenina degenerate into a war of propaganda, each person spewing memorized phrases without even stopping to think about them. John's propaganda sounds more palatable than Lenina's, because Shakespeare's poetic lines put the hypnopaedic messages to shame. Next to Shakespeare, "progress is lovely" sounds cheap and trashy. The juxtaposition of the two contributes to the satirical tone of the novel.

The confrontation between Bernard and the Director illustrates the power of social condemnation. The Director decides to denounce Bernard in front of the other workers in order to make an example out of him. In part, World State members are forced to conform merely by peer pressure and the threat of public shame. Bernard turns the Director's ploy on its head by shaming him with the spectacle of John and Linda. Bernard's willingness to use John and Linda for his own gain further helps to portray him as someone who will do anything to gain social standing. By presenting Linda and John to the Director in front of the workers, he not only manages to save his own position but also to spitefully attack the Director and reduce his social standing.

Lenina's role throughout this chapter is a passive one, for the obvious reason that she is on soma-holiday for most of it. Going on soma-holiday is her only way of dealing with the negative emotions aroused by the Reservation. It is particularly ironic that she goes on soma-holiday in the middle of what should have been a real holiday (her vacation).

CHAPTERS 11–12

SUMMARY: CHAPTER 11

The Director resigns in disgrace, and Bernard is able to keep his job. John, known as "the Savage," becomes an instant society hit. Linda takes soma continually and falls into a half-awake, half-asleep state of intoxication. Bernard experiences unprecedented popularity as John's appointed guardian. He boasts about his thriving sex life to Helmholtz, but Helmholtz responds only with a gloomy silence that offends Bernard. Bernard decides to stop speaking to him. He shamelessly parades his unorthodox behavior, thinking that his popularity as the Savage's discoverer and guardian will protect him. He writes Mond to tell him that John finds "civilized infantility" too easy. Bernard says he agrees with John's verdict. Mond, reading the heretical letter, thinks he might have to teach Bernard a lesson.

The sight of dozens of identical twins in a factory sickens John. With bitter irony, he echoes Shakespeare's line, "O brave new world that has such people in it." He refuses to take soma and visits his mother often. He visits Eton where Alpha children laugh at a film of "savages" beating themselves with whips on a Reservation.

Lenina likes John but cannot tell if he likes her. She takes him to a feely, entitled *Three Weeks in a Helicopter,* that tells the story of a black man who kidnaps a blond Beta-Plus woman for his own enjoyment. John hates the movie, but it reinvigorates his passion for Lenina. His shame at his physical desire overwhelms him. To Lenina's bewilderment, John refuses to have sex with her. He locks himself in his room and reads Shakespeare's *Othello.* Lenina returns to her room and takes soma.

SUMMARY: CHAPTER 12

Bernard arranges a large party of important people, promising them a chance to meet the Savage. But when they arrive, John refuses to leave his room. Bernard is humiliated and embarrassed as all of his guests, including the Arch-Community-Songster of Canterbury, leave in contempt. Lenina is disappointed that she cannot see John again to find out why he behaved so strangely after the feely. The Arch-Community-Songster warns Bernard that he should be more careful in his criticisms of the World State.

Bernard sinks back into his former melancholia now that his newfound success has evaporated. He makes John his scapegoat. Bernard is simultaneously grateful and resentful that Helmholtz gives him the friendship he needs without criticizing him for his earlier unfriendliness. Helmholtz has gotten himself into trouble for reading some unorthodox rhymes to his students at the college. But he is excited to have finally found a voice of his own.

John and Helmholtz meet, and take to one another right away. Bernard is jealous of their affection for one another and wishes he had never brought them together. He takes soma to escape his feelings. John reads passages from Shakespeare to Helmholtz. The poetry enraptures Helmholtz, but when John reads a passage from *Romeo and Juliet* about Juliet's parents trying to persuade her to marry Paris, Helmholtz bursts into laughter. The absurdity of having a mother and father is not the only thing that he finds funny; the fact that anyone would make a fuss over which man a girl should have is even funnier. John locks his book away because Helmholtz's laughter insults and wounds him.

Analysis: Chapters 11–12

In this section John gets a thorough introduction to World State society, which, for the most part, disgusts him. He perceives the culture of the World State to be superficial, inhumane, and immoral.

The relationship between John and Bernard dramatizes the major themes of *The Tempest*. John, who originally believed he would play the part of Miranda, learning to love the new world revealed to him, becomes known as "the Savage" and takes on a role similar to Caliban's; Bernard, by exposing John to civilization and expecting that to win John's everlasting gratitude, plays Prospero to John's Caliban.

The fate of John's mother, Linda, demonstrates what Mustaph Mond meant in suggesting that truth and happiness are incompatible. Everyone but John is content to allow Linda to abuse soma, even though they know it will kill her within a month or two. The doctor's explanation to John demonstrates the World State's callous attitude that human beings are things that should be "used up until they wear out." Just as with manufactured goods, when people get old and worn out, they become disposable. Linda goes on permanent soma-holiday, living out the short remainder of her life in a blissful haze of hallucinations and fantasies.

Bernard's personal reasons for allowing Linda to succumb to soma are even more unpleasant. Everyone in London clamors to see John, but they are equally determined not to see Linda. With Linda safely out of the way, Bernard is free to use John for his own purposes. Through his exploitation of John, Bernard demonstrates that his previous dissatisfaction with the World State had merely stemmed from his desire to enjoy more of its privileges, rather than from any true desire to live as an "adult" (which is how he had presented the matter to Lenina on their first date). When he becomes successful and begins to enjoy the benefits of his Alpha status, he even drops his friendship with Helmholtz, a nonconformist with an increasingly bad reputation. Helmholtz threatens Bernard's newfound success.

The feely that John attends with Lenina involves some old racist stereotypes, but it is quite complicated in its irony. It begins with a scene in which a "gigantic negro" copulates with a blonde woman. This scene in itself would be highly shocking and taboo to Huxley's white, middle-class, early-twentieth-century audience, but so far the feely-goers find it perfectly conventional. They even marvel at the realistic special effects. What the audience within the book finds shocking is when the black man, following a blow to the head that erases his conditioning, kidnaps the blonde for a monogamous three-week sexscapade in a helicopter. It's shocking to them because of the monogamy. Finally, three Alpha males rescue her and order is restored.

This scene reminds the reader of a feature of movies that is even older than Huxley's novel. Theatergoers love to watch characters in movies transgress against the rules that the viewers themselves have to abide by. This vicarious enjoyment is given a thin veneer of respectability through a decorous ending that restores the status quo. But the fact remains that the audience enjoys fantasizing about the transgression. In part, this whole scene is Huxley's joke, but it is also possible that monogamy is not as unusual a fantasy in the World State as we have been led to believe.

The scene in which John reads *Romeo and Juliet* demonstrates the power of conditioning. Even though Helmholtz is fairly unorthodox, he is still a product of World State conditioning. He appreciates the artistic value of Shakespeare's language, but he does not appreciate the drama of Juliet's parents trying to convince her to marry Paris. Because John identifies his desire for Lenina with the love between *Romeo and Juliet,* Helmholtz's laughter insults both his cultural values and his own innermost feelings. But Helmholtz cannot help it; the situations and emotions expressed in the play mean something very different to him than they do to John.

CHAPTERS 13–15

SUMMARY: CHAPTER 13

Henry invites Lenina to a feely, but she declines. He notices that she is upset and suggests that she might need a "Violent Passion Surrogate," or V.P.S. Later she complains to Fanny that she still does not know what it is like to sleep with a savage. Fanny warns her that it is unseemly to become obsessed over one man, and that she should find someone else to take her mind off of him. Lenina replies that she wants only John. Other men simply cannot distract her.

Lenina takes soma and visits John, intending to seduce him. She remarks that he does not seem pleased to see her. John falls to his knees and begins quoting Shakespeare to express his adoration. He speaks about marriage and declares his love for her. She asks why he had not said anything if he had wanted her all along. However, his talk about lifelong commitments and growing old together horrifies her.

Lenina presses her body against his and begins to remove her clothes. John becomes furious and terrified. He calls her a whore and slaps her. She locks herself in the bathroom while John reenacts King Lear's disgusted tirade against womankind and biological generation (*King Lear*, IV.vi.120-127). The phone rings and he answers it. Lenina hears him leave the apartment.

SUMMARY: CHAPTER 14

John hurries to the Park Lane Hospital for the Dying. He whispers impatiently to a nurse that he wants to see his mother. Blushing furiously at his use of the word *mother,* she leads him to Linda's bed. John sits next to her in tears, trying to remember the good times they had together. A troop of eight-year-old Bokanovsky boys gathers around Linda, asking why she is so fat and ugly. John angers the nurse when he strikes one particularly offensive child. She criticizes him for interfering with the children's death conditioning and leads them away.

Linda mistakes John for Popé. He shakes her angrily, demanding that she recognize him as her son. She says his name, starts to recite a hypnopaedic phrase from her childhood, and then begins to choke. He rushes to the nurse in a fit of grief to ask for help, but Linda is dead by the time they get to her ward. John sobs uncontrollably while the nurse worries about the damage done to the children's death-conditioning. She hands out chocolate éclairs to the Bokanovsky twins. One twin points to Linda's body and asks John, "Is she dead?" John pushes him to the floor and rushes out of the ward.

Summary: Chapter 15

In the hospital vestibule, John encounters two Bokanovsky groups of Delta twins picking up their soma rations after their shift. With bitter irony he recalls the lines, "How many goodly creatures are there here! How beauteous mankind is! O brave new world." With "O brave new world" echoing in his head, John cries out for them to stop taking the soma rations. He tells them that it is a poison meant to enslave them and asks them to choose freedom. The man distributing the soma calls Bernard at home. Helmholtz answers the phone and relays the news about John's statements to Bernard. They rush to the hospital together.

The uncomprehending faces of the Delta workers infuriate John. He throws the soma rations out a window. The Deltas rush at him in fury. Helmholtz, who has just arrived, jumps into the fray to help defend John. Bernard hesitates. He knows John and Helmholtz might be killed if he doesn't help, but he is afraid of being killed while trying to help them. He feels shame at his indecision. The police arrive, spraying soma vapor and a powerful anesthetic. Meanwhile, a recorded voice asks why the rioters are not happy together. Before long, the Deltas are crying, kissing one another, and apologizing. Their soma rations are quickly restored. The police ask Helmholtz and John to come quietly. Bernard tries to slip out the door unobserved, but is caught before he can escape.

Analysis: Chapters 13–15

The dramatic riot incited by John is the climax of the novel. John's growing revulsion against everything in the World State finally propels him into a direct confrontation with it, and the authorities are forced to intervene. The events that immediately precede the riot reveal the conflicting forces that culminate in John's outburst.

John's struggle with his physical desires, first introduced on the Reservation, continues when Lenina tries to seduce him. He insists on seeing Lenina as a pure, virginal woman, possessed of complete sexual modesty. To John, Lenina is only an abstract rendering of all the virtuous women he has read about in Shakespeare's works. He struggles with the physical side of sexuality to the point that he wants to repress it entirely. When Lenina makes a pass at him, he calls her a whore for breaking the rules of a moral code she is not even aware of. "Whore" is the only other category that he has to understand Lenina. It is significant that when he locks himself away from Lenina, he chooses to read *Othello*, a play about the doomed relationship between a black African man and a white Venetian woman. Like John, Othello veers between the extremes of perceiving his beloved as a chaste statue and as a whore. It is this misperception that leads Othello to slaughter his wife, not an incompatibility between their two cultures.

John's experience in the Hospital for the Dying demonstrates the dehumanizing logic that the World State applies to death experience. Any tolerance he might once have felt for the practices and people of the World State disappears. He thinks of the Bokanovsky twins as maggots who defile his grieving process. Unfortunately for John, his mother is no help. Drugged on soma, she mistakes him for Popé. John's fury and agony reflects the growing anguish he experiences when he is not recognized in the World State, even by his own mother. The society of the World State names him "the Savage," associating him with a set of stereotypical characteristics. When John visits Eton, he watches a group of children laughing at "savages" on a Reservation performing ceremonial self-flagellation purification rituals. He sees himself reflected in their laughter as a curious, comedic spectacle, not as a human being. Bernard uses John as a curious specimen of "savagery" to attract important people into his own social circle. Helmholtz's laughter at *Romeo and Juliet* makes John recognize that his struggle with his physical attraction for Lenina is a comedic, offensive spectacle even for one of the World State's few nonconformists. Worse yet is the fact that he considers Helmholtz a friend with whom he can discuss his feelings for Lenina. The end result of all these separate episodes is that John acknowledges that he, as an individual, cannot exist within World State society. He is forced either to be a stereotyped representative of "the savage" or to succumb to the warped morals of the World State.

John's attempt to stir the Delta workers into rebellion by throwing away their soma symbolizes his struggle against happiness as the ultimate goal. John would rather see truth and real human relationships—even painful ones—than the near-slavery of soma. His own mother's death by soma is also a contributing factor. Linda and the Deltas use soma to escape all pain and responsibility. This makes them become infantile, something that John points out when he asks the Deltas why they want to be "babies . . . mewling and puking." John's outcry describes the essential logic that produces the "stability" that the World State loves so much. The vast majority of World State citizens remain childlike their whole lives through the use of conditioning, social reinforcement, and soma.

Helmholtz throws himself into the fray when he and Bernard arrive at the hospital, but Bernard hesitates. His hesitation is caused by the conflict between his desire to fit into the World State social machine and his desire to change the way it works. He fears associating himself with the nonconforming blasphemy of John's revolutionary cry and Helmholtz's support of John's actions. Bernard knows that his participation will forever mark him as a dangerous subversive.

Chapter 16

Summary: Chapter 16

The police leave Bernard, Helmholtz, and John in Mond's office. Mond arrives and says to John, "So you don't much like civilization, Mr. Savage." John concedes, but admits that he does like some things, such as the constant sound of music. Mond responds with a quote from Shakespeare's *The Tempest:* "Sometimes a thousand twangling instruments will hum about my ears and sometimes voices." John is pleasantly surprised to find that Mond has read Shakespeare.

Mond points out that Shakespeare is a forbidden text. In response to John's questioning, he explains that such literature is banned for a number of reasons. In the first place, beautiful things, such as great literature, tend to last. People continue to like them even when they become quite old. A society based on consumerism, such as the World State, needs citizens who want new things. Newness is thus more important than intrinsic value, and high art must be suppressed to make room for the new. In the second place, the citizens of the World State would not be able to understand Shakespeare, because the stories he writes are based on experiences and passions that do not exist in the World State. Grand struggles and overpowering emotions have been sacrificed in favor of social stability. They have been replaced by what Mond calls "happiness," by which he means the infantile gratification of appetites.

John is inclined to think that this brand of happiness creates monstrous and repulsive human beings. He challenges the Director, asking whether the citizens couldn't at least all be created as Alphas. Mond replies that the World State has to have citizens who will be

SUMMARY & ANALYSIS

happy performing the functions that they have been assigned, and since Alphas are only happy doing Alpha (i.e., intellectual) work, the vast majority of the population actually has to be degraded and made stupid so that they will be happy with their place in life. He points to an experiment in which an entire island was populated with Alphas, and wholesale civil war quickly ensued, because none of the citizens were ever happy with the distribution of tasks.

Although the World State is a technotopia, meaning that it is made possible by technologies vastly more advanced than our own, Mond explains that even technology has to be kept under rigorous controls for the happy and stable society to be possible. Past a certain point, even labor-saving technologies have had to be suppressed to maintain a balance between labor and leisure. Keeping citizens happy requires keeping them at work for a certain amount of time.

Science has also had to be suppressed to create the happy and stable society. This is particularly ironic because World State citizens are taught to revere science as one of their most fundamental values. However, none of them—not even Alphas such as Helmholtz and Bernard—actually possess any scientific training, so they really don't even know what science is. Mond doesn't explain what it is, although he alludes to his own career as a young scientist who got himself into trouble by challenging conventional wisdom. One can infer that by "science," Mond means the search for knowledge by means of the experimental method. Science cannot exist in the World State because the search for "truth" conflicts with happiness. This is very suggestive, because it implies that the entire society is somehow built upon lies, but he is tantalizingly unclear about what truths and what lies he is talking about.

Mond tells Helmholtz and Bernard that they will be exiled. Bernard begins to beg and plead for Mond to change his sentence. Three men drag him away to sedate him with soma. Mond says that Bernard does not know that exile is actually a reward. The islands are full of the most interesting people in the world, individuals who did not fit in the World State community. Mond tells Helmholtz that he almost envies him. Helmholtz asks why, if he is so envious, he did not choose exile when he was offered the choice. Mond explains that he prefers the work he does in managing the happiness of others.

Mond believes that the islands are a good thing to have around since dissidents like Helmholtz and Bernard would probably have to be killed if they could not be exiled. He asks Helmholtz if he would like to go to a tropical island. Helmholtz says that he would

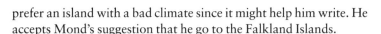

prefer an island with a bad climate since it might help him write. He accepts Mond's suggestion that he go to the Falkland Islands.

_____

ANALYSIS: CHAPTER 16

The conversation between Mond and John is the intellectual heart of *Brave New World*. It is here that the issues implied by the rest of the novel are made explicit, and discussed in an abstract form.

The rationale that Mond provides for suppressing John's beloved Shakespeare gives us a crucial key to understanding the rest of their conversation. The mere fact that Shakespeare is old means that he doesn't contribute to consumer behavior. (Huxley, of course, ignores the fact that people purchase new editions of Shakespeare, Shakespeare college courses, SparkNotes, etc.) While this reason seems superficial in comparison with Mond's more developed arguments, it draws our attention to the fact that consumerism is central to the world of *Brave New World*. Like other dystopias, this novel doesn't simply show us a world that is different from our own, it shows us a world that is a mirror of ours, with the worst features of our world drawn out and exaggerated. One of the central facets of Huxley's novel is directed against the ever-increasing value it places on consumerism.

By showing a world that suppresses institutions and experiences that are sacred in our own world in order to make way for the development of consumer values, Huxley demonstrates a conflict of values that exists in our own society. The "value" that drives the consumer is simply the gratification of appetites. In *Brave New World,* this one value has been developed to the point that people are "adults during worktime," but infants in their leisure time and in their relationships. So Huxley's first criticism of consumerism is that it is infantile—adults should be capable of other things.

If consumption is the "happiness" that Mond refers to in his description of the World State, the other value that his society is predicated on is "stability." In Mond's account, happiness and stability depend upon one another. The stability Mond is talking about is economic stability, the uninterrupted cycle of production and consumption. But emotional, psychological, and social stability are also important, because they all contribute to the first kind of stability.

Mond's argument about the things that must be sacrificed to create a "stable and happy" society may be read, ironically, as an argument that our values are incompatible with consumer behavior and economic stability. The values that Mond sacrifices may be summarized as follows:

FEELINGS, PASSIONS, COMMITMENTS, AND RELATIONSHIPS.
Citizens of the World State have no fathers, mothers, husbands, wives, children, or lovers, because such relationships produce emotional (and therefore social) instability, strife, and unhappiness. While it is easy to think of ways that relationships make people unhappy, it may be difficult for the reader to understand why Mond thinks these relationships fundamentally create instability, when common sense and tradition dictate exactly the opposite, that the family is one of the stabilizing institutions of our society. One answer may be found in Chapter 3, in Mond's lecture to the students. Here he argues that the most dangerous part of passionate commitments to other individuals is the strength of the feeling involved. Moreover, he maintains that all feelings and passions arise from arrested impulses, such as the longing one experiences when one can't immediately have the lover that one wants. This is probably the basis for his idea that the consumer's need for immediate gratification is at odds with long-term human commitments.

EQUALITY.   Mond is quite forthright about the fact that social stability depends upon inequality. Most of society is going to have to perform uninteresting tasks most of the time. This feature of World State society is by no means peculiar to the World State. In fact, it is probably true of every society that has ever existed. It might even be possible to argue that our own society has as much inequality as the World State, and that Mond is just more honest about it, refusing to pay lip service to the ideal that all humans are created equal. However, the complete abandonment of the ideal of equality leads to horrifying results. The majority of human embryos in the World State are altered so that their potential for excellence or growth is stunted. When the comparison is made between the novel's world and our own, we are left with troubling questions rather than distinct conclusions. Given that economic and social stability depends upon an unequal distribution of labor, does this create destructive contradictions with our democratic ideal that individuals are equal? (This theme is clearly indebted to the writing of Karl Marx, whose ideas are part of the intellectual background of this novel. It is no accident, for instance, that the dissident Bernard's last name is Marx.)

TRUTH.   Mond says that science has to be suppressed because a society that is predicated on the search for happiness cannot also be committed to truth. He may mean that science, and the search for truth more generally, has an irresistible tendency to overthrow old, established ways of looking at things. Authority and conventional wisdom both contribute to the stability of society, and in the search for truth both of these are liable to come under interrogation.

ART.   Art is not a consumer product, and great art draws its subject matter from feelings, passions, commitments, and relationships, which are discussed above.

One final category of experiences that are sacrificed in the world state might simply be labeled "problems." Huxley might argue that we value problems (old age, death, doubt, even suffering), because we value the responses that they produce in human beings. These Mond dismisses as the "overcompensation for misery."

One criticism that the reader might be inclined to level at Mond's entire line of argumentation is that it is self-serving. Mond is at the very top of the ruling class and enjoys exemption from the laws that he makes. One could easily dismiss everything he says on the basis that his real interest is the stability of his own position, and not the stability and happiness of his society as a whole. On the other hand, it would be a mistake to simply dismiss his argument out of hand, because it does possess considerable power and subtlety, challenging the reader to dispute it on its own terms.

CHAPTERS 17–18

SUMMARY: CHAPTER 17

As Helmholtz leaves to check on Bernard, John and Mustapha Mond continue their philosophical argument. Whereas their conversation in Chapter 16 covered human experiences and institutions that the World State has abolished, in Chapter 17 they discuss religion and religious experience, which have also been expunged from World State society. Mond shows John his collection of banned religious writings, and reads aloud long passages from the nineteenth-century Catholic theologian, Cardinal Newman, and from the eighteenth-century French philosopher, Maine de Biran, to the effect that religious sentiment is essentially a response to the threat of loss, old age, and death. Mond argues that in a prosperous, youthful society, there are no losses and therefore no need for religion. John asks Mond if it is natural to feel the existence of God. Mond responds that people believe what they have been conditioned to believe. "Providence takes its cue from men," he says.

John protests that if the people of the World State believed in God, they would not be degraded by their pleasant vices. They would have a reason for self-denial and chastity. God, John claims, is the reason for "everything noble and fine and heroic." Mond says that no one in the World State is degraded; they just live by a different set of values than John does. World State civilization does not require anyone to bear unpleasant things. If, by accident something negative occurs, soma is there to take away the sting. Soma, he says, is "Christianity without tears."

> *Christianity without tears—that's what soma is.*
> *(See* QUOTATIONS, *p. 60)*

John declares that he wants God, poetry, real danger, freedom, goodness, and sin. Mond tells him that his wishes will lead to unhappiness. John agrees but does not relinquish his wishes.

SUMMARY: CHAPTER 18

Bernard and Helmholtz say good-bye to John. Bernard apologizes for the scene in Mond's office. John asks Mond if he can go with them to the islands, but Mond refuses because he wants to continue "the experiment." Later, John chooses to seclude himself in an abandoned lighthouse in the wilderness. He plants his own garden and performs rituals of self-punishment to purge himself of the contamination of civilization.

One day, two Delta-Minus workers see John whipping himself. The next day some reporters come to interview him. John kicks one reporter and angrily demands they respect his solitude. The newspapers publish the incident and more reporters flock to John's home. He reacts to them with increasing violence. One day he thinks longingly of Lenina and rushes to whip himself. A man films the scene and releases a sensationally popular feely.

Fans of the feely soon visit John and chant, "We want the whip." As the crowd chants, Lenina steps out of a helicopter and walks toward him, arms open. John calls her a strumpet and proceeds to whip her, saying, "Oh, the flesh! . . . Kill it, kill it!" Fascinated by the spectacle, the crowd mimes his gestures, dances, and sings the hymn, "Orgy-porgy, Orgy . . ." After midnight, the helicopters leave and John collapses, "stupefied by soma" and the extended "frenzy of sensuality." When he awakes the next day, he remembers everything with horror. Having read about the "orgy of atonement" in the papers, a swarm of visitors descends on John's lighthouse, discovering that he has hanged himself.

ANALYSIS: CHAPTERS 17–18

Bernard and Helmholtz leave the scene, and the novel, at the beginning of Chapter 17. By being exiled to the islands, and by accepting their exile, they have lost the fight against the World State. Helmholtz may continue to struggle through his writing. That is the implication of his choice of a particularly harsh environment. But both of them are being physically transported to a location where they can cause little harm to the World State. Only John is left to criticize and debate with Mond.

The discussion of religion carries the book to its most abstract and metaphysical level, and the reader may have difficulty following the thread of the argument from Chapter 16 to Chapter 17, particularly given the long passages of quotation. However, this section goes to the heart of what is wrong with Huxley's dystopia: the fact that nobody conceives of any purpose for existence beyond the gratification of their own appetites. The passage from Newman that Mond quotes suggests that individuals feel the need for religion as they lose the sense that they are in complete control of their own lives, as they experience loss and the weakening that comes with age. The sense that one is not in control of one's life precedes the understanding that one is part of something larger (God's plan). In the World State, no one grows old or experiences loss, so no one ever arrives at religious experience.

In one sense, this can be seen as yet another criticism of consumerism. But Huxley is actually criticizing something larger than 1920s England and America, with its Ford motor cars, diamond rings, and conspicuous consumption. He's criticizing the way philosophers, economists, and social scientists have been thinking about society for almost 400 years—roughly since Shakespeare's day. Before that time, political philosophers from the ancient Greeks onward thought of civil society as serving some purpose. What that entailed varied from culture to culture. For Pericles, an ancient leader of Athens, the purpose of the polis (city-state) was to enable the small minority of free men to perform heroic exploits. In the Middle Ages, the purpose of the nation was frequently conceived as being to carry out God's plan by serving the king, his representative on earth.

Seventeenth-century writers and philosophers such as Thomas Hobbes began to conceive of societies as governed by observable laws, such as the law of supply and demand, which could determine the behavior of large numbers of people. The models of society promoted by Hobbes, and later by the political economists, ultimately generated a sufficient understanding of economic and sociological dynamics to permit governments to effectively promote greater stability, as the government does in *Brave New World*. But these models simplify human life to the mere struggle to survive and escape starvation, and their insights come at the price of the earlier sense that human lives or societies have a greater purpose. And while the lack of a purpose, divine or otherwise, may be a serious flaw in the worldviews of sociology and economics, Huxley observes a much more dangerous tendency within them: the tendency for the government to produce more and more intervention into human life.

The meaning of the novel as a whole lies in Huxley's critique of modernity, characterized by technocratic government, social sciences dedicated to the control of society, and rampant consumerism, and the remarkable observation voiced by Mond in Chapter 3, that everything we think of as fundamentally human—love, passion, desire, art, and culture—comes about because of the experiences of loss and unsatisfied desire. It appears that the point of *Brave New World* is that modernity is developing in a direction that will ultimately change human nature itself. A world in which consumerism is developed to the extent it is in the World State, where desires are immediately gratified, in which "external secretion" is carried to the baby before it has barely begun to cry, would eradicate the most fundamental fact of human existence: its inconvenience.

But at the same time that it points to this conclusion, there are signs throughout the novel that this alteration in human nature has not yet taken place, and perhaps could never take place. Just as we are being told that there are no more jealous lovers, we meet Bernard Marx. Beneath the surface of the "free love" practiced among the higher castes lurks the specter of monogamy and violent passion. Lenina has already dated one man exclusively for far too long, and she indulges with an entire feely-going audience in a scandalous fantasy of monogamy practiced in a helicopter. Routinely, the citizens find themselves having to supplement their soma ration with drugs that replicate pregnancy or violent attachment. And there is the continuing problem of the dissidents who have to be exiled.

The last section of the novel consists of John's departure to the lighthouse to punish himself. His self-flagellation is a desperate attempt to hold onto his own values—truth over happiness among others—in the face of overwhelming pressure from the world around him. Lenina Crowne symbolizes that pressure. John feels a powerful sexual attraction to her, a temptation to give in to the "pleasant vices" that he finds so loathsome and prevalent in World State society. When she arrives along with the chanting crowd, his resolve collapses and, when he wakes the next morning, his realization that he has succumbed to the very thing he was most set against drives him to kill himself.

The language of these chapters continues in the same tone as in the rest of the book: it is a mixture, at times awkward, of didacticism, satire, and farce. The later chapters have a more serious and didactic tone, particularly in the conversation between John and Mustapha, when issues of free will, morality, God, and society come to the fore. In the last chapter, John's frantic self-flagellation contrasts with the superficiality of the gawking reporters and crowds that come to watch him at the lighthouse. The comparison between the two groups symbolizes the basic difference between John and the society in which he finds himself.

Important Quotations Explained

1. Mother, monogamy, romance. High spurts the fountain; fierce and foamy the wild jet. The urge has but a single outlet. My love, my baby. No wonder those poor pre-moderns were mad and wicked and miserable. Their world didn't allow them to take things easily, didn't allow them to be sane, virtuous, happy. What with mothers and lovers, what with the prohibitions they were not conditioned to obey, what with the temptations and the lonely remorses, what with all the diseases and the endless isolating pain, what with the uncertainties and the poverty—they were forced to feel strongly. And feeling strongly (and strongly, what was more, in solitude, in hopelessly individual isolation), how could they be stable?

This passage comes from Chapter 3, when Mustapha Mond is explaining the history of the World State to the group of boys touring the Hatchery. "Mother, monogamy, romance" can be seen as a concise summary of exactly the issues with which John will be most concerned. And "feeling strongly" is what John values most highly, and also what leads to his eventual self-flagellation, insanity, and suicide. Mustapha is saying that by doing away with these things, the World State has finally brought stability and peace to humanity. John's critique of this position is that stability and peace are not worth throwing away everything that is worthwhile about life—"mother, monogamy, romance" included. Another facet of World State philosophy that is encapsulated in this quote is the idea of constructing a world in which human beings have only one way of behaving. The World State is an enormous system of production and consumption in which humans are turned into machines for further production and consumption. The world "allows" them to be happy by creating a system in which not being happy—by choosing truth over soma—is forbidden.

2. Every one works for every one else. We can't do without
   any one. Even Epsilons are useful. We couldn't do without
   Epsilons. Every one works for every one else. We can't do
   without any one. . . .

This quotation comes from Chapter 5, when Lenina remembers
waking up as a small girl and, for the first time, hearing hypnopaedic messages whispered into her ear. She is reminded of the quote
by a discussion with Henry Foster about the fact that all humans,
regardless of caste, become equal after death. This quote illustrates
the power of mind-numbing repetitiveness of the hypnopaedic rules
and beliefs that form the basis of World State society. The message
also highlights the hypocrisy of the conditioning: it may be true that
"every one works for every one else," but it is also true that certain
castes have a much better time of it than others.

3. Ford, we are twelve; oh, make us one,
   Like drops within the Social River;
   Oh, make us now together run
   As swiftly as thy shining Flivver.
       . . .
   Orgy-porgy, Ford and fun,
   Kiss the girls and make them One.
   Boys at one with girls at peace;
   Orgy-porgy gives release.

This song is sung during the Solidarity Service attended by Bernard
in Chapter 5. It gives an example of the banal "religion" the World
State uses to keep its members in conformity with societal rules. The
song's silly wording helps emphasize the triviality of the ceremony.
It also contrasts with the snippets of Shakespeare that John quotes
later in the novel. The theme of anonymity is a metaphor for the
whole of World State society, whose aim is to create humans that
are as indistinguishable from each other as machines made on an
assembly line. The repeated calls to "Ford" also point out the connection to the assembly line. Finally, the last stanza's "orgy-porgy
gives release," like the Violent Passion Surrogate, the Pregnancy
Surrogate, and soma, is a signal that the World State has not been
able to entirely annihilate human nature. There is still some need for
release, some need to experience strong emotions that has not been
entirely wiped out through conditioning. The Solidarity Service is

one of many mechanisms the World State uses to channel strong
emotions in such a way that they present no threat to the power of
the State.

4. A gramme is always better than a damn . . . A gramme in
    time saves nine . . . One cubic centimetre cures ten gloomy
    sentiments . . . Everybody's happy nowadays . . . Every one
    works for every one else . . . When the individual feels, the
    community reels . . . Never put off till to-morrow the fun
    you can have to-day . . . Progress is lovely

These are samples of hypnopaedic sayings that are scattered throughout the novel. Lenina is a continual source of them. In Chapter 6,
she responds to Bernard's soliloquy about the need to be alone with
almost nothing but hypnopaedic phrases. Bernard tells her how
many times, and for how long, each phrase is pumped into the ears
of sleeping children. The irony is that Bernard himself is one of the
people responsible for the hypnopaedic phrases, but when he tries to
escape their logic he is trapped by the people around him who take
every hypnopaedic saying as undeniable truth. The quotes sampled
here reflect some of the basic principles of World State society: the
use of soma to deal with unpleasant emotions; the identification of
happiness as the ultimate goal; the maintenance of the caste system
and the use of conditioning to create workers who enjoy their work;
the prioritizing of the community over the individual; the support
of instant gratification; the promotion of technology and science as
necessary foundations of the good life.

QUOTATIONS

5.   And if ever, by some unlucky chance, anything unpleasant
     should somehow happen, why, there's always soma to give
     you a holiday from the facts. And there's always soma to
     calm your anger, to reconcile you to your enemies, to make
     you patient and long-suffering. In the past you could only
     accomplish these things by making a great effort and after
     years of hard moral training. Now, you swallow two or
     three half-gramme tablets, and there you are. Anybody can
     be virtuous now. You can carry at least half your morality
     about in a bottle. Christianity without tears—that's what
     soma is.

This passage comes from the conversation between Mustapha and
John in Chapter 17. Mustapha is trying to convince John that soma
solves one of humanity's oldest problems: it offers a way to deal with
unpleasant emotions that lead to inefficiency and conflict. He claims
that soma allows everyone to accomplish something that previously
took years to attain. He also makes a connection between religion
and soma. The word *soma* comes from an unidentified, probably
hallucinogenic drug that was used in ancient Indian Vedic cults as
part of religious ceremonies. The soma of *Brave New World* is a
perversion of this ancient drug. Instead of giving insight, it clouds
over the truth. Instead of being used in solemn religious ceremonies,
it is used whenever a slightly unpleasant emotion is felt. Mustapha
describes soma as a tool that allows everyone to be moral, but it can
also be seen as a tool that the State uses to keep its citizens from becoming unhappy enough to try to change the society in which they
live. John rejects Mustapha's "Christianity without tears" as being
too easy, too simple, and too superficial. To John, soma seems to be
little more than an opiate of the people.

QUOTATIONS

Key Facts

FULL TITLE
Brave New World

AUTHOR
Aldous Huxley

TYPE OF WORK
Novel

GENRE
Dystopia

LANGUAGE
English

TIME AND PLACE WRITTEN
1931, England

DATE OF FIRST PUBLICATION
1932

PUBLISHER
Chatto and Windus, London

NARRATOR
Third-person omniscient; the narrator frequently makes
passages of "objective" description sound like the speech or
thought patterns of a particular character, using a technique
usually called "free indirect quotation."

CLIMAX
John incites a riot in the hospital in Chapter 15.

PROTAGONISTS
Bernard Marx, Helmholtz Watson, and John

ANTAGONIST
Mustapha Mond

SETTINGS (TIME)
2540 A.D.; referred to in the novel as 632 years "After Ford,"
meaning 632 years after the production of the first Model T car.

SETTINGS (PLACE)
England, Savage Reservation in New Mexico

POINT OF VIEW
Narrated in the third person, primarily from the point of view of Bernard or John but also from the point of view of Lenina, Helmholtz Watson, and Mustapha Mond.

FALLING ACTION
Chapter 18, in which John isolates himself in a lighthouse and punishes himself; it ends with an orgy and his suicide.

TENSE
Past

FORESHADOWING
Foreshadowing does not play a significant role in the narrative.

TONE
Satirical, ironic, silly, tragic, juvenile, pedantic

THEMES
The use of technology to control society, the incompatibility of happiness and truth, the dangers of an all-powerful state

MOTIFS
Alienation, sex, Shakespeare

SYMBOLS
The drug *soma* is a symbol of the use of instant gratification to control the World State's populace. It is also a symbol of the powerful influence of science and technology on society.

STUDY QUESTIONS

1. *Bernard is criticized by the Director for not acting "infantile" enough. Discuss how and why the World State infantilizes its citizens.*

The World State infantilizes its citizens by allowing them instant gratification and denying them responsibility. It assigns every citizen to a caste and a particular social function before birth, it encourages its citizens to use soma regularly and to seek instant sexual gratification, and it conditions its citizens to have no identity independent of the World State. John compares the dependence of Delta workers on soma to a prolonged childhood. Their reaction to John's call to revolution resembles a childhood temper tantrum. The lifelong process of conditioning socializes the citizens into infantile dependence on the State through the lures of pleasure, security, and happiness. Like children, they are never allowed to make independent moral choices. Instead, these choices are made for them through conditioned, blind obedience to the World State's moral laws. All of this occurs in the name of stability. Infantilization is implemented through scientific discoveries in human psychology, such as Pavlovian theory and hypnopaedia.

2.   *Discuss the relation between the sexes in the World
      State. How do men and women interact? Who holds
      the power in social situations, in the workplace, and in
      the government?*

When the Director gives his new students a tour of the Hatchery at
the beginning of *Brave New World,* it is made immediately clear that
the students are all boys. This is the first of many hints that women
occupy positions of inferior power and status in the World State.
Another clue comes soon after, when we learn that in order to retain
the State's control over reproduction, many of the female fetuses
are sterilized—but none of the male fetuses are. The Malthusian
belt, containing regulation contraceptives, is another example of
the burden placed on women to avoid pregnancies. In sexual relations, men and women seem to be equally promiscuous and equally
free to initiate contact. Lenina is just as ready as Bernard to capital-
ize on the fame brought through association with John by spending time with as many partners as possible. But in work situations
and in the government men are undeniably in charge. Assuming
that Lenina and Fanny are Beta females, there are very few Alpha
women in the novel and none about whom we learn anything significant. The people in positions of power—in propaganda (Bernard,
Helmholtz), in the Hatchery (the Director, Henry), and in the government (Mustapha Mond)—are all male. In the social realm the
relations between the sexes are liberalized, but in the realms of work
and politics the power remains squarely in the hands of men. It is
an open question whether this state of affairs is part of the satirical
target of *Brave New World* or whether it simply reflects the culture
in which the novel was written.

3. *Discuss the parallels between* BRAVE NEW WORLD *and Shakespeare's* THE TEMPEST.

Many critics interpret *The Tempest* as an allegory of imperialism because Prospero decides to raise Caliban and "civilize" him. England has a long history of colonizing "savages" it saw as being in need of "civilizing." In some respects, the World State practices a form of British imperialism. "Civilizing the savages" often involved replacing native languages with English. There are hints that English is the only language in the World State. Polish, German, and French are referred to as "dead languages." Therefore, it seems that the World State has eradicated most other cultures and languages except for a few "Savage Reservations." John identifies with Miranda by quoting her, and, like Miranda, he is raised in isolation from the culture of his parents. However, John resembles Caliban, because he becomes known as "the Savage" when he travels to the World State.

Bernard also parallels different characters from *The Tempest.* Like Prospero's brother, Bernard uses another person to further his own selfish interests. He uses John to acquire greater popularity and status. However, Bernard also becomes John's appointed guardian, so he becomes John's "father" on one level. Bernard's role as guardian is to expose John to "civilization." Therefore, Bernard plays Prospero, as John plays Caliban. London society's reaction to John reproduces the stereotype of the "Noble Savage." This cliché often functioned as a justification for the cultural genocide practiced in British Imperialism. "Civilized" British culture played the parent role to the "child-like savage" by raising him above his "savage, childish" culture. Therefore, the relationship between Bernard and John dramatizes the thematic content of *The Tempest,* as well as the history of British imperialism.

4.   *In what ways does the World State treat people like
     commodities?*

The Predestinators estimate the need for various members of each
caste, and the Hatchery produces human beings to match their math-
ematical figures. This directly follows the economic rules of supply
and demand. Through the Podsnap and Bokanovsky Processes,
the lower castes are mass-produced on assembly lines to satisfy the
needs of a market, just like any other standardized manufactured
good. Linda's doctor and Bernard are content to allow Linda to
abuse soma even though they know it will eventually kill her. The
doctor explains to John that it is better for her to die as quickly and
quietly as possible now that she cannot perform any economically
productive work. The doctor voices the World State's belief that
human beings are things meant to be "used up until they wear out."
Just as with manufactured goods, when people get old and worn
out, they are thrown away. With respect to sexual pleasure, World
State citizens are conditioned to view themselves, and others, as
commodities to be consumed like any other manufactured good. As
Bernard says, Henry and the Predestinator view Lenina as a "bit of
meat," and Lenina thinks of herself "as meat."

How to Write
Literary Analysis

The Literary Essay: A Step-by-Step Guide

When you read for pleasure, your only goal is enjoyment. You might find yourself reading to get caught up in an exciting story, to learn about an interesting time or place, or just to pass time. Maybe you're looking for inspiration, guidance, or a reflection of your own life. There are as many different, valid ways of reading a book as there are books in the world.

When you read a work of literature in an English class, however, you're being asked to read in a special way: you're being asked to perform *literary analysis*. To analyze something means to break it down into smaller parts and then examine how those parts work, both individually and together. Literary analysis involves examining all the parts of a novel, play, short story, or poem—elements such as character, setting, tone, and imagery—and thinking about how the author uses those elements to create certain effects.

A literary essay isn't a book review: you're not being asked whether or not you liked a book or whether you'd recommend it to another reader. A literary essay also isn't like the kind of book report you wrote when you were younger, where your teacher wanted you to summarize the book's action. A high school- or college-level literary essay asks, "How does this piece of literature actually work?" "How does it do what it does?" and, "Why might the author have made the choices he or she did?"

The Seven Steps

No one is born knowing how to analyze literature; it's a skill you learn and a process you can master. As you gain more practice with this kind of thinking and writing, you'll be able to craft a method that works best for you. But until then, here are seven basic steps to writing a well-constructed literary essay:

   1. Ask questions
   2. Collect evidence
   3. Construct a thesis

4. Develop and organize arguments
5. Write the introduction
6. Write the body paragraphs
7. Write the conclusion

---

1. ASK QUESTIONS

When you're assigned a literary essay in class, your teacher will often provide you with a list of writing prompts. Lucky you! Now all you have to do is choose one. Do yourself a favor and pick a topic that interests you. You'll have a much better (not to mention easier) time if you start off with something you enjoy thinking about. If you are asked to come up with a topic by yourself, though, you might start to feel a little panicked. Maybe you have too many ideas—or none at all. Don't worry. Take a deep breath and start by asking yourself these questions:

- **What struck you?** Did a particular image, line, or scene linger in your mind for a long time? If it fascinated you, chances are you can draw on it to write a fascinating essay.

- **What confused you?** Maybe you were surprised to see a character act in a certain way, or maybe you didn't understand why the book ended the way it did. Confusing moments in a work of literature are like a loose thread in a sweater: if you pull on it, you can unravel the entire thing. Ask yourself why the author chose to write about that character or scene the way he or she did and you might tap into some important insights about the work as a whole.

- **Did you notice any patterns?** Is there a phrase that the main character uses constantly or an image that repeats throughout the book? If you can figure out how that pattern weaves through the work and what the significance of that pattern is, you've almost got your entire essay mapped out.

- **Did you notice any contradictions or ironies?** Great works of literature are complex; great literary essays recognize and explain those complexities. Maybe the title (*Happy Days*) totally disagrees with the book's subject matter (hungry orphans dying in the woods). Maybe the main character acts one way around his family and a completely different way around his friends and associates. If you can find a way to explain a work's contradictory elements, you've got the seeds of a great essay.

At this point, you don't need to know exactly what you're going to say about your topic; you just need a place to begin your exploration. You can help direct your reading and brainstorming by formulating your topic as a *question,* which you'll then try to answer in your essay. The best questions invite critical debates and discussions, not just a rehashing of the summary. Remember, you're looking for something you can *prove or argue* based on evidence you find in the text. Finally, remember to keep the scope of your question in mind: is this a topic you can adequately address within the word or page limit you've been given? Conversely, is this a topic big enough to fill the required length?

GOOD QUESTIONS

"Are Romeo and Juliet's parents responsible for the deaths of their children?"

"Why do pigs keep showing up in LORD OF THE FLIES?*"*

"Are Dr. Frankenstein and his monster alike? How?"

BAD QUESTIONS

"What happens to Scout in TO KILL A MOCKINGBIRD?*"*

"What do the other characters in JULIUS CAESAR *think about Caesar?"*

"How does Hester Prynne in THE SCARLET LETTER *remind me of my sister?"*

---

2. COLLECT EVIDENCE

Once you know what question you want to answer, it's time to scour the book for things that will help you answer the question. Don't worry if you don't know what you want to say yet—right now you're just collecting ideas and material and letting it all percolate. Keep track of passages, symbols, images, or scenes that deal with your topic. Eventually, you'll start making connections between these examples and your thesis will emerge.

Here's a brief summary of the various parts that compose each and every work of literature. These are the elements that you will analyze in your essay, and which you will offer as evidence to support your arguments. For more on the parts of literary works, see the Glossary of Literary Terms at the end of this section.

ELEMENTS OF STORY These are the *what*s of the work—what happens, where it happens, and to whom it happens.

- **Plot:** All of the events and actions of the work.

- **Character:** The people who act and are acted upon in a literary work. The main character of a work is known as the *protagonist.*

- **Conflict:** The central tension in the work. In most cases, the protagonist wants something, while opposing forces (antagonists) hinder the protagonist's progress.

- **Setting:** When and where the work takes place. Elements of setting include location, time period, time of day, weather, social atmosphere, and economic conditions.

- **Narrator:** The person telling the story. The narrator may straightforwardly report what happens, convey the subjective opinions and perceptions of one or more characters, or provide commentary and opinion in his or her own voice.

- **Themes:** The main idea or message of the work—usually an abstract idea about people, society, or life in general. A work may have many themes, which may be in tension with one another.

ELEMENTS OF STYLE These are the *how*s—how the characters speak, how the story is constructed, and how language is used throughout the work.

- **Structure and organization:** How the parts of the work are assembled. Some novels are narrated in a linear, chronological fashion, while others skip around in time. Some plays follow a traditional three- or five-act structure, while others are a series of loosely connected scenes. Some authors deliberately leave gaps in their works, leaving readers to puzzle out the missing information. A work's structure and organization can tell you a lot about the kind of message it wants to convey.

- **Point of view:** The perspective from which a story is told. In *first-person point of view,* the narrator involves him or herself in the story. ("I went to the store"; "We watched in horror as the bird slammed into the window.") A first-person narrator is usually the protagonist of the work, but not always. In *third-person point of view,* the narrator does not participate in the story. A third-person narrator may closely follow a specific character, recounting that individual character's thoughts or experiences, or it may be what we call an *omniscient* narrator. Omniscient narrators see and know all: they can witness any event in any time or place and are privy to the inner thoughts and feelings of all characters. Remember that the narrator and the author are not the same thing!

- **Diction:** Word choice. Whether a character uses dry, clinical language or flowery prose with lots of exclamation points can tell you a lot about his or her attitude and personality.

- **Syntax:** Word order and sentence construction. Syntax is a crucial part of establishing an author's narrative voice. Ernest Hemingway, for example, is known for writing in very short, straightforward sentences, while James Joyce characteristically wrote in long, incredibly complicated lines.

- **Tone:** The mood or feeling of the text. Diction and syntax often contribute to the tone of a work. A novel written in short, clipped sentences that use small, simple words might feel brusque, cold, or matter-of-fact.

- **Imagery:** Language that appeals to the senses, representing things that can be seen, smelled, heard, tasted, or touched.

- **Figurative language:** Language that is not meant to be interpreted literally. The most common types of figurative language are *metaphors* and *similes*, which compare two unlike things in order to suggest a similarity between them— for example, "All the world's a stage," or "The moon is like a ball of green cheese." (Metaphors say one thing *is* another thing; similes claim that one thing is *like* another thing.)

---

3. CONSTRUCT A THESIS

When you've examined all the evidence you've collected and know how you want to answer the question, it's time to write your thesis statement. A *thesis* is a claim about a work of literature that needs to be supported by evidence and arguments. The thesis statement is the heart of the literary essay, and the bulk of your paper will be spent trying to prove this claim. A good thesis will be:

- **Arguable.** "*The Great Gatsby* describes New York society in the 1920s" isn't a thesis—it's a fact.

- **Provable through textual evidence**. "*Hamlet* is a confusing but ultimately very well-written play" is a weak thesis because it offers the writer's personal opinion about the book. Yes, it's arguable, but it's not a claim that can be proved or supported with examples taken from the play itself.

- **Surprising**. "Both George and Lenny change a great deal in *Of Mice and Men*" is a weak thesis because it's obvious. A really strong thesis will argue for a reading of the text that is not immediately apparent.

- **Specific**. "Dr. Frankenstein's monster tells us a lot about the human condition" is *almost* a really great thesis statement, but it's still too vague. What does the writer mean by "a lot"? *How* does the monster tell us so much about the human condition?

GOOD THESIS STATEMENTS

Question: In *Romeo and Juliet*, which is more powerful in shaping the lovers' story: fate or foolishness?

Thesis: "Though Shakespeare defines Romeo and Juliet as 'star-crossed lovers' and images of stars and planets appear throughout the play, a closer examination of that celestial imagery reveals that the stars are merely witnesses to the characters' foolish activities and not the causes themselves."

Question: How does the bell jar function as a symbol in Sylvia Plath's *The Bell Jar*?

Thesis: "A bell jar is a bell-shaped glass that has three basic uses: to hold a specimen for observation, to contain gases, and to maintain a vacuum. The bell jar appears in each of these capacities in *The Bell Jar*, Plath's semi-autobiographical novel, and each appearance marks a different stage in Esther's mental breakdown."

Question: Would Piggy in *The Lord of the Flies* make a good island leader if he were given the chance?

Thesis: "Though the intelligent, rational, and innovative Piggy has the mental characteristics of a good leader, he ultimately lacks the social skills necessary to be an effective one. Golding emphasizes this point by giving Piggy a foil in the charismatic Jack, whose magnetic personality allows him to capture and wield power effectively, if not always wisely."

4. DEVELOP AND ORGANIZE ARGUMENTS

The reasons and examples that support your thesis will form the middle paragraphs of your essay. Since you can't really write your thesis statement until you know how you'll structure your argument, you'll probably end up working on steps 3 and 4 at the same time.

There's no single method of argumentation that will work in every context. One essay prompt might ask you to compare and contrast two characters, while another asks you to trace an image through a given work of literature. These questions require different kinds of answers and therefore different kinds of arguments. Below, we'll discuss three common kinds of essay prompts and some strategies for constructing a solid, well-argued case.

TYPES OF LITERARY ESSAYS

- **Compare and contrast**

    Compare and contrast the characters of Huck and Jim in THE ADVENTURES OF HUCKLEBERRY FINN.

    Chances are you've written this kind of essay before. In an academic literary context, you'll organize your arguments the same way you would in any other class. You can either go *subject by subject* or *point by point*. In the former, you'll discuss one character first and then the second. In the latter, you'll choose several traits (attitude toward life, social status, images and metaphors associated with the character) and devote a paragraph to each. You may want to use a mix of these two approaches—for example, you may want to spend a paragraph a piece broadly sketching Huck's and Jim's personalities before transitioning into a paragraph or two that describes a few key points of comparison. This can be a highly effective strategy if you want to make a counterintuitive argument—that, despite seeming to be totally different, the two objects being compared are actually similar in a very important way (or vice versa). Remember that your essay should reveal something fresh or unexpected about the text, so think beyond the obvious parallels and differences.

- **Trace**

    Choose an image—for example, birds, knives, or eyes—and trace that image throughout MACBETH.

    Sounds pretty easy, right? All you need to do is read the play, underline every appearance of a knife in *Macbeth*, and then list them in your essay in the order they appear, right? Well, not exactly. Your teacher doesn't want a simple catalog of examples. He or she wants to see you make *connections* between those examples—that's the difference between summarizing and analyzing. In the *Macbeth* example above, think about the different contexts in which knives appear in the play and to what effect. In *Macbeth,* there are real knives and imagined knives; knives that kill and knives that simply threaten. Categorize and classify your examples to give them some order. Finally, always keep the overall effect in mind. After you choose and analyze your examples, you should come to some greater understanding about the work, as well as your chosen image, symbol, or phrase's role in developing the major themes and stylistic strategies of that work.

- **Debate**

  Is the society depicted in 1984 good for its citizens?

  In this kind of essay, you're being asked to debate a moral, ethical, or aesthetic issue regarding the work. You might be asked to judge a character or group of characters (*Is Caesar responsible for his own demise?*) or the work itself (*Is* JANE EYRE *a feminist novel?*). For this kind of essay, there are two important points to keep in mind. First, don't simply base your arguments on your personal feelings and reactions. Every literary essay expects you to read and analyze the work, so search for evidence in the text. What do characters in *1984* have to say about the government of Oceania? What images does Orwell use that might give you a hint about his attitude toward the government? As in any debate, you also need to make sure that you define all the necessary terms before you begin to argue your case. What does it mean to be a "good" society? What makes a novel "feminist"? You should define your terms right up front, in the first paragraph after your introduction.

  Second, remember that strong literary essays make contrary and surprising arguments. Try to think outside the box. In the *1984* example above, it seems like the obvious answer would be no, the totalitarian society depicted in Orwell's novel is *not* good for its citizens. But can you think of any arguments for the opposite side? Even if your final assertion is that the novel depicts a cruel, repressive, and therefore harmful society, acknowledging and responding to the counterargument will strengthen your overall case.

5. Write the Introduction

Your introduction sets up the entire essay. It's where you present your topic and articulate the particular issues and questions you'll be addressing. It's also where you, as the writer, introduce yourself to your readers. A persuasive literary essay immediately establishes its writer as a knowledgeable, authoritative figure.

An introduction can vary in length depending on the overall length of the essay, but in a traditional five-paragraph essay it should be no longer than one paragraph. However long it is, your introduction needs to:

- **Provide any necessary context.** Your introduction should situate the reader and let him or her know what to expect. What book are you discussing? Which characters? What topic will you be addressing?

- **Answer the "So what?" question.** Why is this topic important, and why is your particular position on the topic noteworthy? Ideally, your introduction should pique the reader's interest by suggesting how your argument is surprising or otherwise counterintuitive. Literary essays make unexpected connections and reveal less-than-obvious truths.

- **Present your thesis.** This usually happens at or very near the end of your introduction.

- **Indicate the shape of the essay to come.** Your reader should finish reading your introduction with a good sense of the scope of your essay as well as the path you'll take toward proving your thesis. You don't need to spell out every step, but you do need to suggest the organizational pattern you'll be using.

Your introduction should not:

- **Be vague.** Beware of the two killer words in literary analysis: *interesting* and *important*. Of course the work, question, or example is interesting and important—that's why you're writing about it!

- **Open with any grandiose assertions.** Many student readers think that beginning their essays with a flamboyant statement such as, "Since the dawn of time, writers have been fascinated with the topic of free will," makes them sound important and commanding. You know what? It actually sounds pretty amateurish.

- **Wildly praise the work.** Another typical mistake student writers make is extolling the work or author. Your teacher doesn't need to be told that "Shakespeare is perhaps the greatest writer in the English language." You can mention a work's reputation in passing—by referring to *The Adventures of Huckleberry Finn* as "Mark Twain's enduring classic," for example—but don't make a point of bringing it up unless that reputation is key to your argument.

- **Go off-topic.** Keep your introduction streamlined and to the point. Don't feel the need to throw in all kinds of bells and whistles in order to impress your reader—just get to the point as quickly as you can, without skimping on any of the required steps.

-----

6. WRITE THE BODY PARAGRAPHS

Once you've written your introduction, you'll take the arguments you developed in step 4 and turn them into your body paragraphs. The organization of this middle section of your essay will largely be determined by the argumentative strategy you use, but no matter how you arrange your thoughts, your body paragraphs need to do the following:

- **Begin with a strong topic sentence.** Topic sentences are like signs on a highway: they tell the reader where they are and where they're going. A good topic sentence not only alerts readers to what issue will be discussed in the following paragraph but also gives them a sense of what argument will be made *about* that issue. "Rumor and gossip play an important role in *The Crucible*" isn't a strong topic sentence because it doesn't tell us very much. "The community's constant gossiping creates an environment that allows false accusations to flourish" is a much stronger topic sentence— it not only tells us *what* the paragraph will discuss (gossip) but *how* the paragraph will discuss the topic (by showing how gossip creates a set of conditions that leads to the play's climactic action).

- **Fully and completely develop a single thought.** Don't skip around in your paragraph or try to stuff in too much material. Body paragraphs are like bricks: each individual

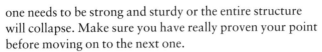

one needs to be strong and sturdy or the entire structure will collapse. Make sure you have really proven your point before moving on to the next one.

- **Use transitions effectively.** Good literary essay writers know that each paragraph must be clearly and strongly linked to the material around it. Think of each paragraph as a response to the one that precedes it. Use transition words and phrases such as *however, similarly, on the contrary, therefore,* and *furthermore* to indicate what kind of response you're making.

---

7. WRITE THE CONCLUSION

Just as you used the introduction to ground your readers in the topic before providing your thesis, you'll use the conclusion to quickly summarize the specifics learned thus far and then hint at the broader implications of your topic. A good conclusion will:

- **Do more than simply restate the thesis.** If your thesis argued that *The Catcher in the Rye* can be read as a Christian allegory, don't simply end your essay by saying, "And that is why *The Catcher in the Rye* can be read as a Christian allegory." If you've constructed your arguments well, this kind of statement will just be redundant.

- **Synthesize the arguments, not summarize them.** Similarly, don't repeat the details of your body paragraphs in your conclusion. The reader has already read your essay, and chances are it's not so long that they've forgotten all your points by now.

- **Revisit the "So what?" question.** In your introduction, you made a case for why your topic and position are important. You should close your essay with the same sort of gesture. What do your readers know now that they didn't know before? How will that knowledge help them better appreciate or understand the work overall?

- **Move from the specific to the general.** Your essay has most likely treated a very specific element of the work—a single character, a small set of images, or a particular passage. In your conclusion, try to show how this narrow discussion has wider implications for the work overall. If your essay on *To Kill a Mockingbird* focused on the character of Boo Radley, for example, you might want to include a bit in your conclusion about how he fits into the novel's larger message about childhood, innocence, or family life.

- **Stay relevant.** Your conclusion should suggest new directions of thought, but it shouldn't be treated as an opportunity to pad your essay with all the extra, interesting ideas you came up with during your brainstorming sessions but couldn't fit into the essay proper. Don't attempt to stuff in unrelated queries or too many abstract thoughts.

- **Avoid making overblown closing statements.** A conclusion should open up your highly specific, focused discussion, but it should do so without drawing a sweeping lesson about life or human nature. Making such observations may be part of the point of reading, but it's almost always a mistake in essays, where these observations tend to sound overly dramatic or simply silly.

A+ ESSAY CHECKLIST

Congratulations! If you've followed all the steps we've outlined above, you should have a solid literary essay to show for all your efforts. What if you've got your sights set on an A+? To write the kind of superlative essay that will be rewarded with a perfect grade, keep the following rubric in mind. These are the qualities that teachers expect to see in a truly A+ essay. How does yours stack up?

- ✓ Demonstrates a thorough understanding of the book
- ✓ Presents an original, compelling argument
- ✓ Thoughtfully analyzes the text's formal elements
- ✓ Uses appropriate and insightful examples
- ✓ Structures ideas in a logical and progressive order
- ✓ Demonstrates a mastery of sentence construction, transitions, grammar, spelling, and word choice

Suggested Essay Topics

1. Discuss the relationship between science, religion, and political power in the World State.

2. What are Mustapha Mond's arguments against freedom? Is there any validity to them? Do you think there is a "winner" of his debate with John?

3. It seems undeniable that most World State members are happy, though people like John, Bernard, and Helmholtz might criticize the quality of their lives. What, then, is wrong with World State society? Discuss the relationship between truth and happiness, and the use of soma?

4. How are the castes distinguished from each other? What is their purpose? Do you think they reflect any aspect of contemporary society or are they simply a hypothetical consequence of a society like the World State?

A+ Student Essay

Is John any freer than the citizens of the World State?

Huxley presents the World State as the extreme culmination of his era's infatuation with technology and comfort. However, we are meant to understand that the same government control that provides subjects with peace and stability also robs them of their essential humanity. The horror of *Brave New World* lies in its depiction of human beings as machines, manufactured on assembly lines and continuously monitored for quality assurance. John, the "savage" from New Mexico, initially seems to represent a kind of pure human being, one whose naturalness contrasts with the mechanization of the World State. However, Huxley goes on to undermine that interpretation, demonstrating not only that John has been socially conditioned just as the World State inhabitants have, but also that his conditioning leads to his downfall.

At first, John seems to represent the fictional philosophical figure known as the noble savage. The noble savage is a primitive human being—usually a man—who grows up isolated in the wild yet possesses an innate sense of morality. John's epithet, "the Savage," deliberately echoes this concept, which tends to portray civilization as a corrupting influence rather than an ennobling one. Writers and thinkers who invoke the noble savage often do so to challenge the cultural arrogance of colonizers, just as John challenges the World State's deeply held belief in the superiority of its system. Crucially, Huxley makes John not a native Indian but a lost descendant of the World State people—visually, physically, and genetically indistinguishable from Lenina, Bernard, and the others. In this way, John seems to function as a sort of scientific "control" in the World State experiment, with all things being equal except the fact that he grew up outside the system.

However, John did not grow up in a vacuum. One of the ironies of the novel is the way Bernard and the others continuously refer to the New Mexico reservation as "the Savage Reservation." In this phrase, we are meant to hear an echo of the European settlers who derided indigenous peoples as savages or barbarians, unable to recognize that the alien-seeming native cultures represented legitimate, if alternate, forms of civilization. Like the Native Americans of our history, the Reservation Indians of *Brave New World* have their own set of rules, customs, and values, which John has internalized. He has been taught to value individual strength and masculinity, and is crushed that he cannot prove himself through the traditional rituals of the tribe. The tribe inculcates a reverence for the divine in John, as well as a belief in committed monogamy and a simultaneous distaste for promiscuity. This proves how powerful an influence the Reservation culture exerts on him, for in adopting their views on religion, love, and individuality, John rejects the teachings of his mother, Linda, one of the few people who shows any concern for him.

In the end, the World State doesn't destroy John for being an intractable non-believer, as we might have expected. Rather, John kills himself when his social conditioning convinces him that he is perverse and wicked. John's notions of love and romance do not represent natural, inherent concepts. Rather, he has learned everything he knows about proper sexual relations from a book—specifically, the collected works of Shakespeare. While we might see John's desire for passion and fidelity as laudable, *Romeo and Juliet* represents just one of the romantic scripts he has learned. At other points in the novel, he identifies more with the title characters of *Othello* and *Hamlet,* who express such deep ambivalence about physical expressions of sexuality that they are driven to murder, suicide, and other brutal acts. In the end, John's inability to reconcile his sexual desires with his romantic ethics leads him to sequester himself in a lighthouse, where he lives in a state of extreme deprivation and self-punishment. John's value system is revealed to be the mirror image of the World State's, which freely celebrates sexuality and forbids romantic love; his self-whippings represent nothing more than violent, physical versions of the technological and rhetorical conditioning practiced by the government.

It would be easy for us to see John's investment in love and individuality as a set of natural principles, since his beliefs seem to reflect our own cultural values. However, to do so would mean perpetuating the same myth employed by World State, which brainwashes citizens into thinking all government-approved feelings are natural, while non-sanctioned desires represent perverse tendencies. In our society, the Reservation, as well as the World State, naturalness represents a supreme value—but each of those communities defines "natural" in a way that suits their needs. Huxley's novel is therefore not a warning to reject technology in favor of natural living, but to carefully examine what "natural" might truly mean.

GLOSSARY OF LITERARY TERMS

ANTAGONIST

The entity that acts to frustrate the goals of the *protagonist*. The antagonist is usually another *character* but may also be a non-human force.

ANTIHERO / ANTIHEROINE

A *protagonist* who is not admirable or who challenges notions of what should be considered admirable.

CHARACTER

A person, animal, or any other thing with a personality that appears in a *narrative*.

CLIMAX

The moment of greatest intensity in a text or the major turning point in the *plot*.

CONFLICT

The central struggle that moves the *plot* forward. The conflict can be the *protagonist*'s struggle against fate, nature, society, or another person.

FIRST-PERSON POINT OF VIEW

A literary style in which the *narrator* tells the story from his or her own *point of view* and refers to himself or herself as "I." The narrator may be an active participant in the story or just an observer.

HERO / HEROINE

The principal *character* in a literary work or *narrative*.

IMAGERY

Language that brings to mind sense-impressions, representing things that can be seen, smelled, heard, tasted, or touched.

MOTIF

A recurring idea, structure, contrast, or device that develops or informs the major *themes* of a work of literature.

NARRATIVE

A story.

LITERARY ANALYSIS

NARRATOR

The person (sometimes a *character*) who tells a story; the *voice* assumed by the writer. The narrator and the author of the work of literature are not the same person.

PLOT

The arrangement of the events in a story, including the sequence in which they are told, the relative emphasis they are given, and the causal connections between events.

POINT OF VIEW

The *perspective* that a *narrative* takes toward the events it describes.

PROTAGONIST

The main *character* around whom the story revolves.

SETTING

The location of a *narrative* in time and space. Setting creates mood or atmosphere.

SUBPLOT

A secondary *plot* that is of less importance to the overall story but may serve as a point of contrast or comparison to the main plot.

SYMBOL

An object, *character,* figure, or color that is used to represent an abstract idea or concept. Unlike an *emblem,* a symbol may have different meanings in different contexts.

SYNTAX

The way the words in a piece of writing are put together to form lines, phrases, or clauses; the basic structure of a piece of writing.

THEME

A fundamental and universal idea explored in a literary work.

TONE

The author's attitude toward the subject or *characters* of a story or poem or toward the reader.

VOICE

An author's individual way of using language to reflect his or her own personality and attitudes. An author communicates voice through *tone, diction,* and *syntax.*

A Note on Plagiarism

Plagiarism—presenting someone else's work as your own—rears its ugly head in many forms. Many students know that copying text without citing it is unacceptable. But some don't realize that even if you're not quoting directly, but instead are paraphrasing or summarizing, *it is plagiarism* unless you cite the source.

Here are the most common forms of plagiarism:

- Using an author's phrases, sentences, or paragraphs without citing the source
- Paraphrasing an author's ideas without citing the source
- Passing off another student's work as your own

How do you steer clear of plagiarism? You should *always* acknowledge all words and ideas that aren't your own by using quotation marks around verbatim text or citations like footnotes and endnotes to note another writer's ideas. For more information on how to give credit when credit is due, ask your teacher for guidance or visit www.sparknotes.com.

Review & Resources

Quiz

1. What is the name of the process that allows the Hatchery to produce many clones from a single egg?

   A. The Podansky Process
   B. The Trotsky Process
   C. The Bokanovsky Process
   D. Centrifugal Bumble-puppy

2. The term for birth in the Hatchery is

   A. Social predestination
   B. Uncorking
   C. Hatching
   D. Decanting

3. How are children in the Nursery conditioned to dislike books and flowers?

   A. By preventing the children from ever seeing books or flowers
   B. By using hypnopaedia to teach them that books and flowers are worthless
   C. By spanking the children when they approach books or flowers
   D. By sounding alarms and shocking the children when they approach books or flowers

4. What two hypnopaedic lessons are the children in the Nursery learning during the boys' tour of the Hatchery?

   A. Elementary Sex and Elementary Class Consciousness
   B. Elementary Fordism and Elementary Class Consciousness
   C. Elementary Sex and Elementary Caste Structure
   D. Elementary Sex and Elementary Soma

5. Why does Fanny try to convince Lenina to be more promiscuous?

    A.   Because she thinks Lenina is lonely
    B.   Because "every one belongs to every one else"
    C.   Because she thinks Henry Foster is treating Lenina poorly
    D.   Because she thinks Bernard Marx is attractive

6. Why are Bernard Marx and Helmholtz Watson friends?

    A.   Both feel alienated from World State society.
    B.   Both are committed to trying to change the World State.
    C.   Both have been persecuted by the World State.
    D.   They are friends for no particular reason.

7. How does the Solidarity Service end?

    A.   With singing and large doses of soma
    B.   With an orgy
    C.   With a sermon from the Community Songster
    D.   With a series of hypnopaedic lessons

8. How does Bernard try to convince Lenina to go on a date with him?

    A.   By inviting her to visit a Savage Reservation
    B.   By telling her that she is "pneumatic"
    C.   By telling her that he loves her
    D.   She does not need to be convinced; he simply asks.

9. Where is the Savage Reservation located?

    A.   New Mexico
    B.   Nevada
    C.   Texas
    D.   Arizona

10. How does Lenina react to observing the Savage religious ritual?

    A.   She is horrified.
    B.   She is fascinated.
    C.   She is sympathetic.
    D.   She ignores it.

REVIEW & RESOURCES

11. Which one of the following World State sayings has to do with soma?

 A. "Everyone is happy now"
 B. "Progress is lovely"
 C. "A gramme is better than a damn"
 D. "Never put off till to-morrow the fun you can have to-day"

12. What is the purpose of the religious ritual performed by the Savages?

 A. To bring rain
 B. To initiate the young men of the pueblo into adulthood
 C. To cleanse the pueblo after the outsiders' visit
 D. To improve community cohesion

13. Why was Linda attacked by the other women of the village in the Reservation?

 A. Because she slept with their husbands
 B. Because she did not speak their language
 C. Because she was from the Other Place
 D. Because she insulted them

14. What was the first book that John read as a child?

 A. *The Complete Works of William Shakespeare*
 B. Milton's *Paradise Lost*
 C. *The Chemical and Bacteriological Conditioning of the Embryo*
 D. Orwell's *1984*

15. What is the name of the feely that John watches on his date with Lenina?

 A. *Three Weeks in a Helicopter*
 B. *A Gramme a Day*
 C. *A New Othello*
 D. *Love in the Sky*

16. After his return from the Reservation with the Savage, what event leads to Bernard's fall from social grace?

   A.   John refuses to meet Bernard's dinner guests.
   B.   John tries to convince a crowd of Deltas not to take soma.
   C.   Lenina abandons him after John refuses to sleep with her.
   D.   Bernard sends Mustapha Mond a letter criticizing the World State.

17. Why is Helmholtz first criticized by the World State authorities?

   A.   He writes a poem about solitude.
   B.   He writes a poem criticizing the World State.
   C.   He reads Shakespeare with the Savage.
   D.   He spends too much time with Bernard.

18. What is the lesson of the Cyprus experiment described by Mustapha Mond?

   A.   A society of Alphas is unworkable.
   B.   Life on a Savage Reservation can destroy any amount of conditioning.
   C.   Happiness is the only criterion for the success of society.
   D.   Soma is a necessary component of a stable society.

19. What did Mustapha Mond do that almost got him exiled to an island?

   A.   He conducted scientific experiments.
   B.   He criticized the World State.
   C.   He wrote poetry.
   D.   He visited a Savage Reservation.

20. Mustapha Mond says that "You can't have a lasting civilization without . . ."

   A.   "plenty of pleasant vices."
   B.   "soma."
   C.   "pre-natal conditioning."
   D.   "stability and happiness."

21. What does "V.P.S." stand for?

    A.   Vigorous Panic Surrogate
    B.   Viviparous Pregnancy Surrogate
    C.   Violent Passion Surrogate
    D.   Vivid Passion Surrogate

22. After retreating to the lighthouse, what does John do that first attracts the reporters?

    A.   He cries for his mother.
    B.   He calls Lenina's name.
    C.   He whips himself.
    D.   He plants a garden.

23. What motivates John's suicide at the end of the novel?

    A.   Linda's death
    B.   His unrequited love for Lenina
    C.   His disillusionment with the "brave new world"
    D.   His participation in a soma-driven orgy

24. Mustapha Mond tells John that civilizations have to choose between God and

    A.   Soma
    B.   Stability and strength
    C.   Machinery and medicine and happiness
    D.   Technology and progress

25. Of the following, who does not sleep with Lenina?

    A.   The Director
    B.   Benito
    C.   John
    D.   Henry

ANSWER KEY

1: C; 2: D; 3: D; 4: A; 5: B; 6: C; 7: B; 8: A; 9: A; 10: A; 11: C; 12: A;
13: A; 14: C; 15: A; 16: A; 17: A; 18: A; 19: A; 20: A; 21: C; 22: C;
23: D; 24: C; 25: A

SUGGESTIONS FOR FURTHER READING

BARFOOT, C. C., ed. *Aldous Huxley between East and West.* New York/Amsterdam: Rodopi, 2001.

BOOKER, M. KEITH. *The Dystopian Impulse in Modern Literature.* Westport, CT: Greenwood Publishing Group, 1994.

————. *Dytopian Literature.* Westport, CT: Greenwood Publishing Group, 1994.

DE KOSTER, KATIE, ed. *Readings on* BRAVE NEW WORLD. San Diego, CA: Greenhaven Press, 1999.

DEERY, JUNE. *Aldous Huxley and the Mysticism of Science.* London: Macmillan, 1996.

HUXLEY, ALDOUS. *Brave New World Revisited.* New York: HarperCollins, reprint edition 2006.

————. *Island.* New York: Harper, 1962.

MECKIER, JEROME. *Critical Essays on Aldous Huxley.* Boston: G. K. Hall & Company, 1996.

MOYLAN, TOM. *Scraps of the Untainted Sky: Science Fiction, Utopia, Dystopia.* Boulder, CO: Westview Press, 2000.

ORWELL, GEORGE. *1984.* New York: Knopf, 1992.

REVIEW & RESOURCES

SparkNotes Literature Guides

1984
The Adventures of Huckleberry Finn
The Adventures of Tom Sawyer
The Aeneid
All Quiet on the Western Front
And Then There Were None
Angela's Ashes
Animal Farm
Anna Karenina
Anne of Green Gables
Anthem
As I Lay Dying
The Awakening
The Bean Trees
Beloved
Beowulf
Billy Budd
Black Boy
Bless Me, Ultima
The Bluest Eye
Brave New World
The Brothers Karamazov
The Call of the Wild
Candide
The Canterbury Tales
Catch-22
The Catcher in the Rye
The Chocolate War
The Chosen
Cold Sassy Tree
The Color Purple
The Count of Monte Cristo
Crime and Punishment
The Crucible
Cry, the Beloved Country
Cyrano de Bergerac
David Copperfield
Death of a Salesman
Death of Socrates
Diary of a Young Girl

A Doll's House
Don Quixote
Dr. Faustus
Dr. Jekyll and Mr. Hyde
Dracula
Edith Hamilton's Mythology
Emma
Ethan Frome
Fahrenheit 451
A Farewell to Arms
The Fellowship of the Rings
Flowers for Algernon
For Whom the Bell Tolls
The Fountainhead
Frankenstein
The Giver
The Glass Menagerie
The Good Earth
The Grapes of Wrath
Great Expectations
The Great Gatsby
Grendel
Gulliver's Travels
Hamlet
The Handmaid's Tale
Hard Times
Heart of Darkness
Henry IV, Part I
Henry V
Hiroshima
The Hobbit
The House on Mango Street
I Know Why the Caged Bird Sings
The Iliad
The Importance of Being Earnest
Inferno
Invisible Man
Jane Eyre
Johnny Tremain
The Joy Luck Club
Julius Caesar

The Jungle
The Killer Angels
King Lear
The Last of the Mohicans
Les Misérables
A Lesson Before Dying
Little Women
Lord of the Flies
Macbeth
Madame Bovary
The Merchant of Venice
A Midsummer Night's Dream
Moby-Dick
Much Ado About Nothing
My Ántonia
Narrative of the Life of Frederick Douglass
Native Son
The New Testament
Night
The Odyssey
Oedipus Plays
Of Mice and Men
The Old Man and the Sea
The Old Testament
Oliver Twist
The Once and Future King
One Flew Over the Cuckoo's Nest
One Hundred Years of Solitude
Othello
Our Town
The Outsiders
Paradise Lost
The Pearl
The Picture of Dorian Gray
Poe's Short Stories
A Portrait of the Artist as a Young Man

Pride and Prejudice
The Prince
A Raisin in the Sun
The Red Badge of Courage
The Republic
The Return of the King
Richard III
Robinson Crusoe
Romeo and Juliet
Scarlet Letter
A Separate Peace
Silas Marner
Sir Gawain and the Green Knight
Slaughterhouse-Five
Song of Solomon
The Sound and the Fury
The Stranger
A Streetcar Named Desire
The Sun Also Rises
A Tale of Two Cities
The Taming of the Shrew
The Tempest
Tess of the d'Urbervilles
The Things They Carried
The Two Towers
Their Eyes Were Watching God
Things Fall Apart
To Kill a Mockingbird
Treasure Island
Twelfth Night
Ulysses
Uncle Tom's Cabin
Walden
War and Peace
Wuthering Heights
A Yellow Raft in Blue Water

Visit sparknotes.com for many more!